FIGHTING
INVISIBLE
TIGERS

Stress Management for Teens

FIGHTING INVISIBLE TIGERS

Stress Management for Teens

REVISED & UPDATED THIRD EDITION

Earl Hipp

WITHDRAWN

free spirit
PUBLISHING®

Library of Congress Cataloging-in-Publication Data

Hipp, Earl, 1944-
    Fighting invisible tigers : stress management for teens / Earl Hipp. — Rev. & updated 3rd ed.
    p. cm.
    Includes index.
    ISBN-13: 978-1-57542-282-4
    ISBN-10: 1-57542-282-4
    1. Youth—United States—Life skills guides—Juvenile literature. [1. Stress (Psychology)] I. Title.
    HQ796.H495 2008
    155.5'18—dc22

2007044631

At the time of this book's publication, all facts and figures cited are the most current available. All telephone numbers, addresses, and Web site URLs are accurate and active; all publications, organizations, Web sites, and other resources exist as described in this book; and all have been verified as of March 2008. The author and Free Spirit Publishing make no warranty or guarantee concerning the information and materials given out by organizations or content found at Web sites, and we are not responsible for any changes that occur after this book's publication. If you find an error or believe that a resource listed here is not as described, please contact Free Spirit Publishing. Parents, teachers, and other adults: We strongly urge you to monitor children's use of the Internet.

The perfectionism scale on page 101 has been reprinted with permission of *Psychology Today*.

Edited by Douglas J. Fehlen
Illustrated by Tyson Smith

10 9 8 7 6 5 4 3
Printed in the United States of America
S18860509

Free Spirit Publishing is a member of the Green Press Initiative, and we're committed to printing our books on recycled paper containing a minimum of 30% post-consumer waste (PCW). For every ton of books printed on 30% PCW recycled paper, we save 5.1 trees, 2,100 gallons of water, 114 gallons of oil, 18 pounds of air pollution, 1,230 kilowatt hours of energy, and .9 cubic yards of landfill space. At Free Spirit it's our goal to nurture not only young people, but nature too!

Free Spirit Publishing Inc.
217 Fifth Avenue North, Suite 200
Minneapolis, MN 55401-1299
(612) 338-2068
help4kids@freespirit.com
www.freespirit.com

green press
INITIATIVE

Printed on recycled paper
including 30%
post-consumer waste

Dedication

This book is dedicated to all those young people who are fighting invisible tigers without help and support.

Acknowledgments

Writing is only one piece of bringing a book into the world. It also takes a publisher who "gets it," contributors, editors, artists, printers, and office and warehouse people all doing their parts to put this book in your hands. It's this whole crew I want to thank for their special skills and contributions. I feel truly blessed to have them on my team.

In addition, my very special thanks go out to:

My publisher, Judy Galbraith, for her ongoing commitment to the young people she serves. She is one of my heroes and a great role model.

My editor, Douglas Fehlen, for his keen eye, helpful perspective, and patient encouragement.

All the teachers and school staff who daily give their best so kids can learn.

The helping professionals who work with young people in so many different roles, but with the common goal of creating better lives for kids and families.

All the young people who took a risk to so freely share their comments in this book.

All of my family and friends, my safety net of support, who remained available and "on my side" throughout the writing of this book.

My sweet partner in life, Gwen, for her help and patience as I work on making my dreams come true.

Contents

Introduction

Do you ever feel worried or stressed out? If so, you're not alone. Everyone feels upset or overwhelmed at times.

Facing one tough challenge at a time might be okay, but that's not how life usually works. Instead, one thing piles on top of another. In a single week you might have to finish a big project, take a few tests, perform in the school play, put in hours at your job, and do a bunch of other things. At the same time, you might also be dealing with situations that come up at home or troubles you have with friends.

Stress is the feeling you have when facing many challenges at the same time. Imagine every worry, tough homework assignment, health concern, relationship problem, computer glitch, and disagreement is a separate rubber band around your head. That would be very uncomfortable, right? But it can get worse. As more stressors show up, more rubber bands get layered on until your head is completely covered. The pressure you feel on the inside of that ball of rubber bands is stress.

Knowing where to start fixing things can be difficult because stress comes from all of the pressures you have in your life. It's normal to feel anxious and uncomfortable every day when you're feeling stressed—like something is wrong—even though you can't say exactly what it is.

Stress Overload

Dealing with a lot of stress can make people feel cornered—like there's nowhere safe to turn. Making good decisions under this kind of pressure can be difficult. Instead of calmly coming up with solutions to a problem, feelings of tension or anger can get in the way and cause people to do things that make a situation worse.

Fighting Invisible Tigers

When you're stressed out, it can feel like you're in a thick jungle with lots of dangerous tigers—ferocious, hungry, but invisible tigers. You can't see them, but you can sense them quietly stalking you.

Imagine . . .

You're alone in a steamy jungle. You've been hacking through it for days while huge mosquitoes chomp at your flesh. Weird noises and strange smells fill the air. Every now and then you hear a deep, menacing growl . . . and you worry what's going to happen next.

Now imagine living with this fear every day—always watchful, always on edge and ready to react in an instant. That's how a person who doesn't know how to handle stress can feel. Being on guard every minute takes an enormous amount of energy—whether it's watching for real tigers or invisible ones in the form of tests, homework, bullies, friendship fallouts, or other challenges. Constant worry about what might happen next is exhausting and can push you to your limit.

The bad news is you can't keep stress out of your life completely—situations will come up that cause you to feel uncomfortable, frustrated, or overwhelmed. The good news is you can learn more about stress and positive ways to deal with the challenges and hard times. You can learn how to fight the invisible tigers when they do show up.

Stress Is Serious Business

High levels of stress over long periods of time can have severe effects. You might begin to feel aches and pains and get sick more often. Your performance at school and in other activities may suffer. Stress can also affect your moods, you might start to feel angry, sad, lonely, or depressed.

How Can This Book Help?

The goal is to help you stay healthy, meet challenges, feel great about yourself, and make the most of your life. *Fighting Invisible Tigers* offers ideas you can use to really understand stress and handle it in positive ways:

"Stress 101: The Lowdown on Invisible Tigers" has information on stress and its physical and emotional effects. You'll read about some of the unhealthy ways people deal with feeling overwhelmed, and learn the important difference between short-term coping techniques and real stress management.

In "10 Tiger-Taming Techniques" you'll learn about important skills you can use to manage stress—helpful strategies you can start using right now to relieve some of the pressure you feel and prepare for future challenges.

Finally, **"First Aid for Tiger Bites"** has helpful suggestions for when you feel like you've hit your limit. If you're feeling upset or overwhelmed right now, you can check out this section (page 123).

Reading this book may not make you an expert tiger tamer overnight, but practicing the skills can help you make your invisible tigers seem smaller and much less ferocious. I sincerely hope that with less stress, your heart, mind, and spirit will be more open to the joys of life.

Good luck, and my very best wishes go with you on your adventure.

Earl Hipp

P.S. I like hearing from my readers. If you're willing to share, I'd enjoy hearing about how you're doing and what you're learning. I may even be able to help others by sharing your thoughts in my books and presentations. Feel free to send your comments or questions to me in care of:

Free Spirit Publishing
217 Fifth Avenue North, Suite 200
Minneapolis, MN 55401-1299

Or email me at help4kids@freespirit.com.

Stress 101:
The Lowdown on
Invisible Tigers

Stress may seem like a modern phenomenon, but actually it's been around for millions of years. Even in the times of cave-dwelling humans, people struggled with problems that made life complicated, difficult, and frightening—fires that wouldn't start, bad weather, spoiled meat, damp caves, unruly neighbors, and the challenge of simply surviving. But the most serious stressors for cave dwellers were the wild animals that saw them as, well, lunch.

The Fight-or-Flight Response

On a nice day in the jungle, for example, a huge hungry saber-tooth tiger could suddenly leap at the cave dwellers. Because most tigers are in no mood for conversation, these early humans learned to react instantly to either attack the cat or run for safety. This required a finely tuned nervous system that could mobilize the body into what we now call the fight-or-flight response. Over millions of years, the people with the best fight-or-flight skills lived on to tell stories around the fire, and the others . . . well, let's just say they didn't make it home for dinner.

While most of us will never have to face real tigers, the world we live in can feel every bit as threatening as the one that cave dwellers experienced. Think about it for a moment: There are a lot of situations that can make us feel upset or seriously threatened.

The Power of Fight-or-Flight

The fight-or-flight response gets your body ready to do battle or run like the wind at the first hint of danger. It is so sensitive that simply thinking about hungry tigers or any other frightening things can get you fired up and ready to go.

"The environment is being destroyed—will we even have a place to live in 50 years?"

"Since we moved to this town, I haven't been able to make friends."

"I lost my cell phone—it had all of my numbers in it."

"My life is drama central. Justine hates me and Maria says I stepped in on her crush."

"Someone was stabbed in my neighborhood and I'm afraid to walk alone."

"I'm overweight and everybody in my class ignores me."

"There's a guy at school who thinks I'm his personal punching bag."

"My friend Sam is into some really bad things."

"What am I going to do when I finish school?"

"I get sad when I see starving people on TV."

"I have a huge test next week that makes up half my biology grade."

"My parents had a major fight—Mom moved out."

Some challenges definitely are more difficult to deal with than others. But the problem is, whenever you're up against something, anything that makes you feel worried or threatened—even if you're just thinking about it—your body still responds as if it's meeting a hungry tiger. At the first hint of trouble, the alarm goes off, and instantly your body gets ready to fight or run away.

During times of high stress, the fight-or-flight response causes many physical changes in your body—all at the same time—and if you don't understand what's happening, it might feel like you're having a serious medical problem.

Effects of Fight-or-Flight

Here are some of the ways your body might react to stress:

Your heart pounds. The body needs all the oxygen-rich blood it can get, and it needs it in a hurry, so your heart pumps harder and faster. Your breathing also speeds up to make more oxygen available.

Your hands and feet become cooler. Small capillaries in the hands and feet constrict to force blood toward the brain and into the large muscles used for running and fighting.

Stress Affects Your Mind

Stress not only causes changes to your body, but it can also cause your brain to short-circuit. When you feel stressed, the decision-making part of your brain goes offline and stress chemicals flood your system. So what does this mean? When you're stressed, you are a lot more likely to make bad decisions or do things that can make a situation worse. Teens are especially affected by this process because their brains are developing very quickly and changing during adolescence.

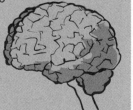

There is a rush of warmth to your face. The carotid arteries in the neck open up to allow more blood to the brain, sometimes causing the cheeks and ears to turn pink. You might get a pressure headache.

Your mouth gets dry and your stomach feels upset. During fight-or-flight, the digestion process shuts down so blood is available for the body's largest muscles.

You feel restless. Glands and organs produce chemicals—including adrenaline—that help prepare the body to move. You may feel tingly or have "butterflies" in your stomach.

Your hands sweat. Anticipating the extra heat that running and fighting generate, the body turns on its climate-control system and produces moisture on the surface of the skin. Evaporation of this moisture creates a cooling effect.

Find Out More

Stress Relief: The Ultimate Teen Guide by Mark Powell. Full of information on stress, this book offers ideas for handling tough situations. It also describes meditation and breathing exercises for calming down.

TeensHealth (www.teenshealth.org). This Web site has a lot of advice on dealing with stress as well as many other health concerns. Visit the site to find articles, teen stories, and resources.

Too Stressed to Think? A Teen Guide to Staying Sane When Life Makes You Crazy by Annie Fox and Ruth Kirschner. Stress affects everyone, but that doesn't mean it has to take over your life. This book provides background on what makes stress difficult to handle and offers practical tips for staying sane.

Short- and Long-Term Stress

The fight-or-flight response can take a lot out of you because battling tigers—real or invisible—is a whole body experience. Fortunately, these moments of intense stress don't usually last very long. After the immediate danger of a stressful event passes, the body gradually calms down and enters a period of rest and recuperation before returning to a normal state. This type of an event is called short-term stress.

Short-term stress usually passes pretty quickly and without a lasting impact. But what happens if you have a lot of things causing stress in your everyday life? What if your life is full of invisible tigers—large and small—that don't ever seem to go away?

When you're experiencing many stressors over long periods of time, your body may not have time to calm down, rest, and recuperate. Because you want to keep going, it's easy to adapt to higher and higher stress levels without realizing it. You might think you are doing okay, but you're actually living with an unhealthy amount of stress. This is why long-term stress can be so harmful—people don't realize the toll it's taking until they reach their limit.

Seriously stressed people are usually trying to stay on top of things—even when they feel stalked by invisible tigers. But high levels of stress can be overwhelming. You might try harder and harder to keep up with all the challenges you are facing while—without realizing it—gradually losing physical energy, the ability to think clearly, and your performance edge. It's like chopping wood with an ax and never taking time to sharpen the blade, or trying to surf the Web using an Internet connection that is getting slower and slower. Eventually, things that were easy become more difficult.

Stress and Pimples

While many effects of stress are quite serious, others can simply be annoying. For example, some researchers believe there is a link between stress and pimples. In the largest-ever study done on acne and stress, teens with high-stress lives were 23 percent more likely to have their acne get worse. Apparently, when you're stressed, your skin knows it, and may react with angry eruptions.

Get Help!

If you feel like you're reaching your limit, it's important to talk with someone you trust—like a parent, teacher, or friend—right away. The person you share with might have solutions to challenges you haven't thought of. See "First Aid for Tiger Bites" (pages 123–126) for more ideas about what to do when you're feeling overwhelmed.

Coping Strategies

Life is full of situations to deal with—responsibilities at home, schoolwork, figuring out where you fit in, friendships. And then there are the unexpected stressors that can happen at anytime. So how do you cope? What is "coping" anyway?

Think of coping as the short-term approach to dealing with the feeling of being stressed. Coping behaviors don't fix the problems that cause stress, but they can give you temporary relief from anxious feelings. There's nothing wrong with most coping activities— things like watching TV or napping—as long as they aren't harmful and don't go on forever.

What are some of these short-term actions people use to cope with feelings of stress? There are three basic categories.

1. Distraction—Or, I'll deal with it later.

"When I need a breather, I go for a bike ride."
—Sarah, 12

"At the end of a long day, I like to check out my Web page. It helps me decompress all the stuff that's happened to me."—Mario, 14

Distractions are the most common coping activities. They're usually pretty harmless and include things like using the Internet, reading, eating, or playing video games—pretty much any activity that allows you some time away from stressors. Distractions can be good for short-term relaxation and can even be productive. For example, taking a short break for a snack while studying is a way to briefly get away and come back with clearer focus. But taking too many breaks—such as to text your friends or chat online—won't get your work done and can increase the stress you feel.

Distractions help you avoid feeling stressed for a little while, but the more you use them to procrastinate, the more the stress you're avoiding creeps to the surface. That's often when people move on to the next level of coping.

2. Avoidance—Or, I might deal with it . . . sometime.

"My friends and I are pretty intense basketball players. We could play hoops all night."—Kwame, 13

"I admit it—when I don't want to do something, I go online. It's weird because I seem to get lost in time. Sometimes I look at the clock and it's hours later." —Brie, 14

Think of avoidance as distractions carried to the extreme—like when watching a little TV becomes watching every night for hours and hours. It's when a simple activity starts to take up more and more of your time and energy and causes you to put off dealing with things you're worried about or don't want to do. Unfortunately, this can lead to a *vicious circle* of behavior. That's when distractions pretty much take over your life. For example, hanging out with friends is great and can be an effective way to de-stress. But spending all your time with friends—day and night, in person or online—to distract yourself from difficulties at home or school shows a pattern of avoidance.

Overachievement. Some serious avoidance activities can appear to be positive. For example, people who are bothered by some deep problem may get super-involved in activities and overachieve to try to overcome negative feelings they have. They may excel in the classroom, be star athletes, and stay active in many school clubs. People who do this may seem to be totally together, but all of their activity is really a way to avoid dealing with the main problem.

People who overachieve often don't have the time, energy, or awareness to address the root feelings of stress. This can quickly become a vicious circle—the more time spent staying busy, the worse a person might feel. The more badly they feel, the more active they become. Around and around it goes in a spiral, down into a deeper and deeper hole of isolation. Vicious circles can close in from all sides, growing tighter and tighter. Because the people affected are so concentrated on trying to keep it all together, they may not notice things steadily getting worse.

Procrastination. Pretty much everyone puts off boring or hard tasks from time to time. Some of the smartest, most motivated, and successful people are known (or secret) procrastinators. When you occasionally put things off, you can pretty much survive—even if it means a late night of studying at some point. But continuously using procrastination as an avoidance strategy can invite a vicious circle—one where mountains of things pile up for you to do, and you develop more drastic ways to avoid facing it all. Before long, you might have a stress-filled mess of missed deadlines, poor excuses, and confused priorities.

Procrastination is most dangerous when it becomes a way of avoiding the hardest parts of life—like tough problems at home, breakdowns in your relationships, or difficulties at school. When you put off dealing with really hard problems or emotions, you can find yourself living with high levels of anxiety or confusion. You might end up feeling panicked or isolated until something inside you breaks. It's like slowly shaking a can of soda. Things look the same from the outside, but when you pop the tab—POW—you have one big, nasty mess on your hands.

Illness. Another avoidance strategy is using sickness to avoid the hard parts of life. Many students learn as little kids that illness is an acceptable reason to miss school—wasn't it nice to sleep in and chill out in front of the TV because you were "sick"? While it's tempting to take advantage of this strategy today, it's a risky play to use illness to avoid difficult situations.

For example, one of the main reasons students avoid school is out of fear—fear that they will be hurt, teased, or harassed by others. Bullying is a serious problem in many schools, but it is not an excuse to drop out. It can be hard to speak up about the girl sending nasty texts about you or the guy who puts your head into lockers, but that's the best approach. What is the alternative? To avoid dealing with it by faking aches and pains to stay home? Each time you skip you fall further behind in your classes. Meanwhile, the main source of your stress—the situation at school—goes unresolved and adds to the tension you feel.

Sleep. It's normal to want to sleep in on Monday morning or to take an occasional nap. Most teens don't sleep the nine to ten hours each night their bodies need, so getting some solid sack time is actually a good thing. It can be a problem, however, if you stay in bed to hide out from stress-causing situations rather than reach out for help.

Stress and Sickness

Faking illness can turn into a vicious circle of real, stress-driven health problems. Headaches, digestive problems, allergies, muscle pain, high blood pressure, eating disorders, chronic fatigue, and depression are only some of the many serious stress-related conditions.

Sleeping for 12 hours night after night or not leaving your bed on weekends isn't healthy, because your problems can become more serious the more you sleep. Sleeping doesn't fix the problems you're facing, so they are still there when you wake up. As the challenges you face become more serious, you may want to sleep more until the effects of stress actually make it difficult to get out of bed.

Isolation. As your world gets more stressful and you feel tiger breath on the back of your neck, it's natural to want to retreat to a place where you feel safe. Withdrawing from the world for a while to regroup can be very good for you. But when you close your door and never come out, healing and restful withdrawal can become dangerous isolation. Even if you don't have a room of your own, you can shut out other people by ignoring them, not being around, or by refusing to engage in any way. If a little time out becomes a need to always be alone, you may be caught in a vicious circle of isolation.

When you use isolation as a way to avoid invisible tigers, you lose the support and objectivity everyone needs when they're dealing with hard situations. When you're alone with your thoughts, negative or destructive thinking can sabotage your self-esteem and leave you feeling hopeless or depressed.

3. Escape—Or, I don't want to deal with it . . . ever.

"I made a bad mistake a couple years ago when things were intense. I'm in juvenile detention now and I miss being home."—Bobby, 15

"Sometimes I wish I could drop out—of school, of life, everything."—Cham, 14

Severe Escapist Behaviors

- skipping or dropping out of school
- running away from home
- using alcohol or other drugs
- addiction to food, sex, gambling, or the Internet
- over-involvement in academics, sports, and other activities
- hurting other people
- lying to people as a way of life
- injuring yourself or attempting suicide

Escapist behaviors can occur when you reach the limit of your ability to cope with the world around you, when you're at the edge of what you can handle. You've done the best you can to deal with the challenges you're facing, using the tools you have, but it's not enough. You're scared, overwhelmed, maybe embarrassed you can't handle things, and you feel like all you can do is check out. Engaging in any escape behaviors is a sign you have lost your way, and you should get some help immediately.

When you're feeling overwhelmed, hopeless, and at your limit, escape can feel like the only option. But escapist behaviors always make a bigger mess of your life and don't solve the underlying issues. They also generate mountains of additional problems that can burden you for years . . . maybe the rest of your life.

Relying on coping activities is like using your finger to plug a leak in a dam. It works for a while, but then the growing pressure behind the dam breaks through in another place, and another, and another. . . . At some point, you run out of fingers. While these coping activities can be helpful in the short term, they are not a replacement for stress-management techniques you'll read about in the next section. For now, let's take a look at some myths about stress—and the final word on the subject.

Get Help!

If you're involved in or moving toward any escapist behaviors, find someone you can talk to about what's going on. Remember: Asking for help when you're up against more than you can handle is not a sign of weakness. It's a sign of strength and courage to make things better. You might start the conversation by saying, "I'm having trouble with some parts of my life. Can I talk with you about how I'm feeling?" "First Aid for Tiger Bites" (pages 123–126) has more ideas for getting help.

10 Myths About—and the Last Word on—Stress

Some myths about stress actually make it more difficult for you to successfully manage the challenges you're facing. Believing any of these myths is a sure way to let invisible tigers gain on you.

10 Myths About Stress

Myth #1. I must be crazy for thinking and feeling the way I do. You're not crazy. Stress can cause anyone to have frightening thoughts and uncomfortable feelings. It's not that anything is wrong with you, just that your life is full of challenges and you're still learning the best ways to manage the stresses in your life.

Myth #2. I need to handle these fears and problems by myself—if I ask for help it proves I'm not smart or good enough. Actually, the opposite is true. Trying to handle tough situations alone most often leads to bigger problems. Reaching out for help when you need it is always the smartest way to stay healthy and perform at your best.

Myth #3. No one will understand how I feel. It's true that some of the important people in your life may not exactly understand your worries or know how to help, but someone will. If one person doesn't take you seriously, reach out to others until you find someone who does.

Myth #4. I can think my way out of feeling bad. Unfortunately, this isn't true. Feelings are nonintellectual, which means no amount of thinking can help you change them. When we're thinking about feelings, what we're usually doing is worrying. Worrying doesn't solve problems and only makes you feel worse. Like setting a music player to play the same song over and over, worrying is just repeating thoughts about bad things that might happen. These fears can wear you down.

Myth #5. If I keep busy, I'll feel better about myself. Staying active can help you to avoid dwelling on some small worries. But the big problems—those responsible for the major stress in your life—won't go away until you face and deal with them in a constructive way. In fact, staying super active can lead to vicious circles (see page 13) and gradually make you feel worse over time.

Myth #6. If I can get through today, tomorrow is bound to be better. Maybe, and maybe not. It's possible that letting some time pass will make your concerns seem smaller or less serious. But it's also true that avoiding problems as a long-term solution can lead to harder times. Living with stress every day also leaves you with less energy and sharpness to deal with the day's challenges. The best strategy is to deal with negative feelings as soon as you're aware of them.

Myth #7. I should be able to figure out things by myself. Who says? Being in the middle of a stressful situation is the hardest time to know what to do to make things better. Trying to figure it out alone cuts you off from the knowledge, experience, and support of others. That's why getting the outside perspective of a counselor, family member, or other trusted adult can put you on the path toward feeling better.

Myth #8. Life is so serious. Life does have many serious moments, but not balancing the pressure of these times with fun, rest, and relaxation will only make the hard times that much harder. You deserve to feel good about yourself and the life you have.

Myth #9. All I need is to be left alone for a while. Being alone can be helpful sometimes. But if your way of dealing with major stress in your life is to be by yourself and avoid talking to anyone, you can quickly get out of touch with reality and your support system.

Myth #10. I don't have time to try or practice stress-management techniques. The basics of stress management relate to activities you're probably already doing every day—things like eating well, getting exercise and rest, and having fun. Learning about a few tiger-taming skills—like time management, relaxation exercises, and goal setting—can help you have even more quality time.

And Now, the Absolute, Bottom-Line Truth About Stress . . .

There is no stress in the world.

That's right: There is no stress in the world. Surprised? Think about it. Where would you go looking for it if you wanted to find stress? Los Angeles? The Gobi Desert? Google? The bottom of your book bag? Chengtu, China? Stress just isn't anywhere "out there."

Stress is something that happens inside people—inside of you. It's the result of how you think and feel about your experiences and challenges you face. To understand this better, imagine yourself in these two situations:

1. You're at the zoo having a great time when a person on the staff asks you to help feed the tigers—even though you have no training with animals. You look at the tigers, the tigers look at you (lunch!). Somehow you're not all that excited to help feed the tigers.

2. You're at the zoo minding your own business when you're asked to help feed the tigers. Luckily you've graduated from Zoo Keeper School with high honors. You have all the skills and expertise you need to do the job, and you confidently enter the tiger sanctuary.

In each scenario, the tigers are the same. What's different is how you perceive them. And that depends on the skills you bring to the situation. For example, a test you haven't studied for probably makes you anxious. But the same test, after solid preparation, can seem like a piece of cake. It's the same with a lot of life's stressful moments. Having the right skills can make the difference between stress overload and really enjoying your life. The next section explains some of these very important tiger-taming skills.

10 Tiger-Taming

Listening to music, shopping at the mall, and other coping activities can take your mind off worries for a short time, but any challenges you face are still there when you push the stop button or finish shopping. Stress-management skills, on the other hand, can help you eliminate some of the stress in your life and give you tools to handle future pressures. What are stress-management skills? This section features 10 Tiger-Taming Techniques.

#1 Get Moving
Ideas for keeping active to stay on top of stress—page 25.

#2 Fight Stress with Food
Nutrition information you can use to feel your best—page 33.

#3 Find Your Calm Center
Relaxation skills that are good for your body and mind—page 41.

#4 Stand Up for Yourself
Assertiveness skills that can help reduce the stress you feel—page 57.

#5 Weave a Safety Net of Support
Suggestions for building strong relationships with friends and family—page 67.

Techniques

#6 Take Charge of Your Life
How to set goals and work toward making your
dreams come true—page 77.

#7 Get Time on Your Side
Using time-management tips to sidestep stress—
page 87.

#8 Risk Trying New Things
Positive ways to challenge yourself and keep moving
forward—page 97.

#9 Stand on Solid Ground
Advice for making decisions that are right for you—
page 107.

#10 Choose the Upside View
Learning to see what's good about yourself and the
world around you—page 116.

Maybe you already use some of these techniques,
others might not be familiar to you. This section gives
you the opportunity to try all of the techniques and
find those that work best for you.

"Sometimes when my brothers are fighting and yelling, I take myself out for a long walk to calm myself down . . . even if it's raining. I always feel better afterward."
—Pat, 13

"After my workout, I feel like I have more energy for the rest of the day. If I miss my routine, I start to feel sluggish and I have trouble getting things done."
—Karna, 14

"Sports are my outlet—I couldn't live without them."
—Rebecca, 16

"I go for a swim when I start to feel tense. Every time I hit the pool, I lose a lot of the negative junk in my head and my mind becomes more clear."
—Kevin, 15

Get Moving

Regular physical activity is one of the best stress-management skills. It's especially helpful during high-pressure times when your body is filled with fight-or-flight chemicals and raring to go. By doing almost any physical activity you use up some of the cortisol and other stress chemicals your body produces. If you're not active at these times, you can feel nervous, restless, uncomfortable, and even ill.

Some Benefits of Physical Activity

The positive health effects of regular physical activity do not end at relieving your body of stress-producing chemicals. Exercise also produces other chemicals—including endorphins—that help you feel good. Just putting your body in motion can help you feel more mellow and improve your mood. That's why after an especially hard day, a little physical activity can help you slow down, relax, and even sleep better.

Physical activity also has a huge impact on your health. In fact, being regularly active can change your entire body chemistry. As your fitness level improves, your body gets better at turning calories into energy—which means you store less fat on your body and use more of the energy stored in the foods you eat. The overall impact: You're not as hungry, you eat less, and you naturally crave foods that are better for you.

Your heart, lungs, muscles, and other vital parts of your body also become stronger and more efficient when you're active—researchers have shown that regular physical activity can add years to your life. Over time, feeling good about how you treat your body can also lead to higher self-esteem and feeling like you're taking charge of your life.

The FIT Formula for Physical Activity

How can you tell whether you're active enough? One way to get on the right track is to create a personalized activity program. You can do this using the FIT Formula. This formula helps you build a physical activity program that's right for you.

Frequency

The U.S. federal government recommends at least one hour of physical activity most days of the week, preferably daily. The good news is that this activity doesn't have to be a chore. Qualifying activities

FIT Formula

F stands for **Frequency**—the number of times per week you do your activity.

I stands for the **Intensity level** you choose for the activity.

T stands for **Time**—how long your activity sessions last.

can be just about anything that gets you moving. In fact, one health campaign focused on teens playing with a yellow bouncy ball—not too intense. If playing with a yellow ball isn't your thing, then walk, swim, dance, skateboard, bike, shoot hoops, throw a frisbee, or do any other activity that's easy to make a habit.

Intensity

You may be tempted to go faster or farther or compete with others—or compete with yourself—by constantly pushing to exceed previous results. Wanting to perform well is okay, but pushing yourself too hard can lead to fatigue or injury. And too-high fitness expectations can become another source of stress in your life. If you always overdo the intensity of your activity, it can become an uncomfortable chore.

The best way to avoid burning out or injuring yourself is to find a level of intensity that is just right for you. One rule of thumb easy to remember: If you can carry on a conversation during your routine, you're probably at a good intensity level. Inviting a friend to join you for a workout is a great way to monitor your intensity—and to keep you motivated.

A more scientific way to gauge the intensity of your activity session is to monitor your target heart rate (THR) while you are active. Your ideal THR is the specific pulse rate at which you receive the maximum benefit from your activity to build fitness and reduce stress. Contrary to popular belief, working harder is not necessarily better. You can figure out your target heart rate using this formula:

THR Formula

$$\frac{(220 - \text{your age}) \times 70\%}{6} = \text{Your THR for a 10 second count}$$

The top part of the formula determines your target heart rate per minute. You divide it by six because when you check your pulse, you only count for 10 seconds. After that, a healthy heart is already beginning to return to its normal, non-active rate.

To find out if you're close to your THR, spend about 20 minutes at your chosen physical activity. Then check your pulse rate using your wrist or the carotid artery along the side of your neck. Look at a watch and count the beats for 10 seconds to see if you're in the zone . . . or at least within a few beats of your ideal number.

- If you're above your target heart rate or out of breath, you're probably pushing yourself too hard. Try slowing down the next time you work out.

- If you're below your target heart rate, you might be taking it too easy. To get full benefit from your activity, try increasing your pace before checking your THR again.

- If you are at or close to your target heart rate, you've found the intensity level you want to maintain during your activity sessions.

Exercising at a pace that's comfortable for you will help you stick with an activity and avoid injury. At the right intensity level, your activity should be an enjoyable, relaxing, and stress-free part of your day that you look forward to.

The "Runner's High"

Have you ever heard of the term runner's high? It's the description given to feelings of joy or elation people sometimes experience during and after working out. Exercise affects hormone levels in your body, and your brain releases endorphins and other chemicals that elevate your mood and can lead to feelings of pleasure.

Time

To get the most out of any physical activity session, you need to keep your heart going at or near your target rate for a minimum of 20–30 consecutive minutes. A "work-hard-then-take-it-easy" approach won't give you the maximum benefit of activity. And don't forget to spend a few minutes stretching and warming up before an activity and cooling down afterwards to keep your flexibility and avoid injury.

If you're not sure how to start your activity program, you might get some inspiration and guidance from a health or physical education teacher. It's also a good idea to check in with your doctor.

Find Out More

President's Challenge (www.presidentschallenge.org).
A program sponsored by the U.S. government, the President's Challenge encourages teens to participate at any activity level to improve their fitness. Visit the Web site for fitness calculators, activity logs, and other tools to help you establish your physical activity program and to track your progress.

Teenage Fitness: Get Fit, Look Good, and Feel Great **by Kathy Kaehler.** This book highlights the author's struggles with body image and gives teens tools they can use to keep their focus on fitness—not the "perfect body." Specific suggestions for workout routines make this a practical guide to staying fit.

"I've been overweight since fourth grade. Only with the help of a nutrition program have I started to feel healthier."
—**Marcos, 13**

"I used to think that I didn't have time for real meals and healthy snacks. Now that I'm used to feeling better from eating real food, I don't think I could ever go back."
—**Jillian, 15**

"Junk food is everywhere around you. How can you *not* eat it?"
—**Carl, 14**

"It's harder to find good food, but the extra effort is worth it. Decent meals keep my body healthy and let me focus at a higher level."
—**Riyanna, 16**

Fight Stress with Food

If you want to be a high-energy and active person who can manage stress, you'll need to put the right fuel in your tank. Eating a lot of different healthy foods—like fruits, vegetables, and whole grains—gives you the vitamins, minerals, protein, and other nutrients your body needs to function at its highest levels. Many other food options, sometimes those easiest to find, aren't good for your health. A poor diet can lead to conditions like diabetes and obesity, and actually increase feelings of stress.

Why Is Eating Healthy So Important?

All of the cells in the body are affected by the foods you eat. Every bodily action, from the way an injury heals to how well you're able to focus, is dependent on the performance of these cells.

For example, the 100 billion cells in your brain rely on proteins and vitamins to communicate and work together. The levels of these and other nutrients in your diet can affect how well you're able to concentrate during a stress-packed test. Healthy foods also give you the energy you need to perform at a high level. The bottom line: Your cells can tell the difference between what's healthy and what's junk, and you're not going to be at your best if you don't treat them right.

The typical teen needs between 2,200–2,800 daily calories, including increased amounts of calcium, protein, iron, and other important nutrients to be healthy. Growth spurts can affect the number of calories you need, so it's important to discuss diet with a school nurse or doctor at regular checkups.

Bad Diet Habits

Fresh Fruits and Veggies

Fresh produce is better for you than processed foods made in a factory. Fruit and vegetable food products are often high in fat, sugars, and artificial additives.

While vegetables, fruits, and other healthy foods can raise your body's defenses against stress and help you think more clearly in tough situations, other parts of your diet can decrease your ability to function under pressure. At the same time you're eating healthy foods, it's also important to cut down on bad health choices as much as possible.

Caffeine

Caffeine is a very common drug found in coffee, tea, soda, energy drinks, and many other beverages. It can also be "hidden" in some foods, including chocolate and ice cream—and even in aspirin, cold capsules, cough syrups, and other over-the-counter medicines.

Caffeine creates an artificial and temporary lift for people who are stressed-out and tired. It feels like energy, but it's very different from the kind you get from good food or physical activity. Like any mood-enhancing drug, the quick "up" creates the illusion you're feeling better than you actually are.

Why can caffeine be a problem? Because it creates a physical reaction similar to the fight-or-flight response. Caffeine causes your body to release more of the stress hormone cortisol—essentially a bump in caffeine causes a bump in the stress you feel. A little can actually improve performance, but it's easy to overdo it. Instead of helping you feel on top of your game, caffeine can leave you feeling anxious and jittery. The drug can turn up the volume on your worries so that every moment you're looking over your shoulder for invisible tigers.

The side effects of too much caffeine are very similar to the symptoms of stress overload. Because of this, drinking caffeine is like drinking fear in small doses. Too much and you'll sense invisible tigers all around you. Unfortunately, caffeine can also be addictive and—like any addiction—the more you use it, the more it takes to produce the same effect. When you set out to eliminate or cut down on caffeine there can be some serious withdrawal symptoms, including major headaches. If you feel like you need a boost of energy and don't go for the caffeine, you may find yourself unconsciously drawn to another bad choice.

Possible Side Effects of Caffeine

- restlessness
- nervousness
- irritability
- shaking
- sleeplessness or nightmares
- sweaty hands or feet
- irregular heartbeat
- nervous or upset stomach
- intestinal disturbances
- panic attacks (sudden feelings of overwhelming anxiety that come without warning or any obvious reason)

Sugar

Like caffeine, sugar is also very common in our diets. It's often overlooked in foods because it can be listed under many different names—including glucose, sucrose, fructose, and corn syrup. These and other processed forms of sugar are chemically potent and your

body absorbs them into the bloodstream quickly. This gives you a "sugar high," a sensation that can give you a lift—for about an hour—before the effect wears off and you experience an energy crash. For this reason, large doses of sugar can generate mood swings where you feel up one moment and tired or crabby the next.

What causes the sugar high? Simply put, the sudden boost in blood sugar surprises your pancreas. The average pancreas is generally a calm and stable organ. It maintains a normal level of sugar in the blood stream. You can imagine the excitement when all of a sudden—bam!—incoming sugar in mega-doses sets off an alarm. While you're getting the rush of sugar-driven energy, your pancreas jumps into high gear, secreting insulin to absorb the excess sugars and carry them off to the liver.

Sometimes, however, your pancreas puts out too much insulin and removes too much blood sugar, which can send you back into the sleepy head-nodding doldrums. You might begin to feel tired or cranky, and soon the vending machine is calling to you from down the hall. If you give in and buy another sugary drink or candy bar, you may find yourself strapped into the front seat of the Sugarcoaster. Up (sugar rush), down (sugar crash), up (sugar rush), down (sugar crash)—and on and on. The problem is each down takes you deeper than the last, and by the end of a day, you're wiped out.

When the Sugarcoaster leaves you feeling low, a caffeine fix might seem like a good idea. But combining a lot of sugar and caffeine can be a prescription for exhaustion and confusion. One chemical (sugar) picks you up and later drops you off a cliff into a mild depressive state. The other (caffeine) strings you along with artificial energy that can give you headaches and cause you to exaggerate fears. While caffeine and sugar in moderate quantities usually do not lead to significant health problems, cutting down on them can definitely help you stay on top of stress.

Sugar Fix

- The average person in the United States consumes about 225 pounds of sugar each year.

- One can of regular cola contains the equivalent of about half of a sandwich bag full of white sugar.

- People in the United States drink over 50 million gallons of soda each year.

- Elevated soda consumption has been linked to increased risk of tooth decay, obesity, diabetes, and the bone disease osteoporosis.

- Sports drinks associated with health and fitness are often full of sugar.

Why It Can Be Hard to Eat Well

Unfortunately, many of us have very busy lives and don't make healthy eating a priority. Over the course of a stressful day, it can seem like there's no time for nutritious meals. Instead of finding food that's good for you, it's easier to stop at fast-food chains or convenience stores. It's not hard to find potato chips, candy bars, soda, or high-fat burgers and fries, but these on-the-go foods have very limited nutrients and often have ingredients that can be bad for your health.

Important!

All this talk of food, don't forget about the water! Did you know that water makes up about 70 percent of our body weight? It's true. Most of our organs are made up of tissues with high water content, and maintaining that percentage is important toward our overall health. Blood is almost completely made up of water, and it serves many vital purposes—including maintaining a regular body temperature, clearing the body of wastes, and ensuring organs receive important nutrients. That's why, in addition to a healthy diet, drinking enough water also is important. How much exactly do you need? Most experts believe eight to ten glasses a day will help you keep your body functioning at a high level. (Of course, you may need more on days when you're very physically active.) If you have trouble drinking enough water, try to make it a point to have a glass every couple hours. Carry a water bottle with you and refill it as needed. Your body will thank you for it!

Eating well is not always easy. Many schools are trying to give students healthier options, but some still have vending machines with sugary foods and carbonated drinks. It can also be extra hard for you to have a healthy diet if proper nutrition isn't a priority for your family.

Consider the hunt for great food to be a positive challenge. Arm yourself with information, then do your best to make good choices. Sometimes the best choice will mean avoiding unhealthy chemicals and other times it might mean ordering a salad at a fast-food restaurant instead of fried food. In addition to putting healthy fuel in your tank and consuming fewer stress-enhancing chemicals, you can feel good knowing that you're treating your body right.

Find Out More

Fueling the Teen Machine by Ellen Shanley and Colleen Thompson. A pair of registered dieticians offer advice on healthy eating habits. Covering a broad range of topics, the book's food recommendations are specific to teens' rapidly growing bodies.

MyPyramid.gov (www.mypyramid.gov). Visit this Web site to learn more about healthy eating options. You can enter your age, height, weight, and activity level to receive a tailor-made food plan for a healthy diet.

Nutrition.gov (www.nutrition.gov). This Web site from the U.S. Department of Agriculture is a one-stop source of information on getting essential nutrients from your diet, handling weight issues, planning for meals, and more. Look for links to information specifically for teens.

"My mom taught me how to meditate. I'm learning how to detach from my stressful thoughts."
—Jakob, 13

"Breathing is like the simplest thing in the world—you can't not do it. But I never realized how I breathe can make such a difference in how I feel."
—Sadie, 15

"Relaxation at the end of a long day helps me leave stress behind."
—Noah, 16

"Who would have thought that relaxing is really about focusing?"
—Deb, 14

#3
Find Your Calm Center

We all have moments when life seems overwhelming, when we feel uncertain or insecure. It's as if we're alone on a tiny lifeboat caught in a huge hurricane in the ocean. We get rocked by waves of emotion, tossed around by all the things we have to do, and almost blown over by our worries and fears. In those moments, it's natural to wonder if we can handle it, if we'll even survive.

When you're being tossed around in the stormy waves of life, another important set of skills can help you find the eye of the hurricane—the calm place right in the middle of all the chaos, commotion, and confusion where you can rest up and recover. Relaxation techniques can help you find that calm place.

What Are Relaxation Techniques?

When you hear the word "relaxation," you might think of playing video games or some other activity that gives you a break from the stressors in your life. But real relaxation is actually *non-doing*. Relaxation techniques allow you to be physically still while maintaining an alert, but neutral mental focus. Some of the actions you might think of as "relaxing" may feel good, but they are coping behaviors—ways to avoid the feeling of being stressed. Real relaxation provides a form of deep rest for your body and mind and helps you feel relief from any invisible tigers chasing you.

Knowing how to relax and find your calm center helps keep your body and mind in tip-top, tiger-taming condition. If you're always tense, your muscles never get a break. This constant stress can fatigue your entire body and make you feel aches and pains. At some point you begin to feel tired all over and even start to lose flexibility so that simple, everyday activities seem harder and take more energy.

Similarly, constantly thinking or worrying about all the challenges in your life can lead to mental fatigue and exhaustion. Without the ability to relax and regroup in a calm place, you might begin to feel "brain fade"—that's when you lose some of your ability to think clearly and generate creative ideas. Relaxation skills can help you pull yourself back together so you can feel calm and capable.

Brain Waves

The billions of cells in your brain use electricity to communicate. This electrical communication can be measured by high-tech sensors and shows up as visible wave forms on a monitor. Your brain has different wave patterns, depending on whether you're stressed, calm, or asleep. Researchers have shown that relaxation exercises promote an alpha wave pattern—a pattern that shows a state of alertness and physical and mental relaxation.

Coping or Real Relaxation?

Can you spot the true relaxation techniques in this list?

1. Watching TV
2. Going for a walk
3. Focusing on your breathing
4. Taking a nap
5. Gradually tensing and relaxing your muscles
6. Reading a book
7. Meditating
8. Chatting with a friend online

If you guessed 3, 5, and 7 are the relaxation techniques, you're right. Everything else, no matter how pleasant, falls in the category of coping strategies. While watching TV, reading, and chatting online can all be fun and give you a break from the hard stuff, they're not relaxation techniques because your brain is busy and your mental focus isn't neutral. Going for a walk can be a nice break, but it's not a relaxation exercise because you're not physically still, you have to watch out for traffic, and your mind can easily wander into worrying. Sleeping isn't a relaxation technique either because it isn't a controlled state and you're not alert. Nightmares are proof that sleep isn't always relaxing.

Coping strategies make you feel better temporarily because they mask or distract you from anxiety and tension. But the only real relaxation techniques on the list are focused breathing, meditation, and muscle relaxation—techniques where you are calm, alert, and have a neutral mental focus.

Focused Breathing

Your body and mind influence one another in powerful ways. Your thoughts and feelings affect your body chemistry. At the same time, how you feel physically influences your attitude and mood. Bringing body and mind into balance with each other helps you be more relaxed, rested, and in control of how you're feeling. Focused breathing is an easy way to create calmness in the center of a stress-filled day.

When you're nervous, excited, or angry, your breathing is more rapid and tends to move up in your chest. The result is short, shallow breaths that don't provide your body with the oxygen it needs. When you're relaxed and at ease, on the other hand, your breathing is slower and deeper. Slow, deep, regular breathing is the physical expression of a calm mind.

What is your breathing like right now? Because you're sitting down and reading a book, your breathing is probably deep and slow. The next time you're feeling stressed, check your breath. It will most likely be a lot faster and shallower. Just sitting and worrying about something (or *many* things) can change your breathing. The good news is you can learn to control your breathing to achieve a calmer mental state—even during times of high stress. The following exercise can help you learn how.

Important!

Until you master all of the steps in these exercises, you might want to have someone read them to you. For example, you and a friend could take turns reading and relaxing. You can also find mp3 files of the relaxation scripts at www.freespirit.com. Search for *Fighting Invisible Tigers* to find files you can download to your phone or media player.

Getting Ready

- Find an appropriate location to perform this exercise. You'll need a comfortable place to lie down where it's quiet and you're not likely to be disturbed.

- Loosen any tight clothing or belts that might restrict your breathing. You may also wish to remove your shoes for comfort.

- Commit to doing the Focused Breathing exercise until it's over. Stopping early won't allow you to get the full benefit.

- You may want to tell the people around you what you're doing—you don't want them to panic if they walk in and see you laying on the floor and not moving!

- Cycle through all of the steps of the exercise 3–4 times. Your breathing should deepen and slow so that you feel calmer. Allow your breathing to quicken to its normal rate before getting up.

Focused Breathing Exercise

1. Sit or lie in a comfortable position.

2. Keeping your mouth closed, inhale and exhale deeply through your nose a few times to settle into the moment.

3. Place your right hand on your stomach, near your belly button, and your left hand at the top of your chest.

4. Do not try to control your breathing yet. Just notice where in your body your breath is located.

5. Take a long, slow, deep breath into your chest. Your left hand should rise with the inhalation, but your right hand should remain pretty still.

6. Pause briefly, keeping your chest full, and then release and allow a slow exhale through your nose.

7. Repeat this "chest breathing" three times.
   Breathe in, chest rises . . . hold . . . release and exhale.

- Notice which muscles are involved, the sensation of fullness at the pause, and the feeling of relaxation that comes with the slow, deliberate release of air.
- In . . . hold . . . release.
- In . . . hold . . . release.

8. Take a break. Stop controlling your breath for a few rounds, and wait till your breathing finds its own rhythm and natural location.

9. Again take a long, slow, deep breath, but this time, direct the inhalation into the bottom of your diaphragm (just below your rib cage), hold, and release. Your right hand near your belly button should rise and fall while your left hand stays pretty much still.

10. Repeat this "belly breathing" three times.
    - Breathe in, right hand rises . . . hold . . . release.
    - In . . . hold . . . release.
    - In . . . hold . . . release.

11. When you're done, take another break and give your breathing a chance to return to its natural state.

12. Now, keeping both your hands in place, combine all of the breathing movements into one slow, continuous, four-count exercise, like this:
    - Count "one" and breathe into your belly so your right hand rises. Pause for a mini-second.
    - Count "two" and breathe into your chest so your left hand rises. Pause for a mini-second.
    - Count "three" and begin a controlled, gradual exhalation from your belly so your right hand lowers. Pause for a mini-second.
    - Count "four" and slowly release the remaining air in your chest so your left hand lowers.

13. When you feel you have completely exhaled, pause for a split-second before you start the cycle again.

14. Repeat this four-count breathing pattern for two to three minutes. You can use this rhythmic chant, saying to yourself: inhale belly, inhale chest, exhale belly, exhale chest.

Focusing on your breathing and counting like this may seem difficult or feel strange at first, but with a little practice, the activity can feel natural and very soothing. As you get more comfortable with the exercise, you may want to lengthen your sessions. Once you're familiar with this way of creating the peaceful eye in the center of the storm, you'll be able to visit the calm place whenever you're beginning to feel overwhelmed by stress.

Sitting in the Calm

Just as your heart beats endlessly and automatically, day in and day out, your mind is "always on"—it's a thinking machine that produces an endless stream of thoughts. If you don't believe it, here's an experiment to prove it: Set this book down for a moment, close your eyes, and turn off your brain. Ready? Stop thinking right . . . now!

Did it work? Of course not. Shutting off your brain is simply impossible. No matter what you do, your thoughts continually lurk in the background. This includes your fears and worries—your own thoughts can become some of your worst invisible tigers.

Although you can't stop the flow of your thoughts, you can learn how to detach from them and focus your attention on something else. For example, right now, move your attention to the bottom of your right foot. Did you suddenly become more aware of what was going on there? Now, shift your attention to the sensation of your hand holding this book. There it is. You can suddenly feel the book even though you weren't noticing it before.

The attention rule goes like this: What we pay attention to gets louder or more prominent in the moment. The same is true for your thoughts. Sometimes we're thinking about what's outside of us, and other times we're busy with our inner thoughts. Our thoughts shift fairly easily, but wherever our focus lands, that's what commands our attention.

The primary challenges of relaxation and meditation skills are learning to be physically still, focusing your attention on something other than your thoughts, and then keeping it there. This meditation exercise can help you learn to detach from your thinking machine and simply sit in calm.

Getting Ready

- Choose a time and place you're likely not to be disturbed. Remember to turn off your cell phone and eliminate other possible distractions.

- Commit to the exercise. Decide before you start how long the session will last. In the beginning, 3–5 minutes is enough. Later, you may want to lengthen your sessions. Whatever length you choose, set a timer and don't stop until time is up.

- During the activity, don't control your breathing. Let your breathing find a depth and rhythm that's naturally comfortable.

- Don't move. You should keep your body still for the entire session. If you focus your attention on what your body is doing or feeling, you will become distracted from the experience.

Sitting in Calm Exercise

1. Place a firm chair in front of a blank wall.

2. Sit on the chair facing the wall with your back relaxed but straight. This position may feel uncomfortable at first but it will become more comfortable over time.

3. Put your feet flat on the floor.

4. Fold your hands in your lap or place them palms-down on top of your thighs.

5. Keep your head up and pull your chin in a little to keep your neck straight.

6. Keep your eyes open, but look down at about a 45-degree angle at the blank wall. Don't tilt your head—just look down.

7. When you have the position right, focus on your breathing. Don't try to control it in any way—just keep your mouth closed and give your attention to the passing of the inhalations and exhalations through your nose.

8. When you're ready to begin, silently count "one" on the next inhalation and "two" on the exhalation, "three" on the next inhalation and "four" on the exhalation . . . and so on up to "ten." When you reach "ten," start over with "one" on the next inhale. . . .

Roadblocks to Sitting in Calm

When you set out to sit still in calm, many distractions can come up. Here are some you might encounter and instructions for dealing with them.

Roadblock #1: Your Rebellious Mind. Your mind may not appreciate your attempts to control your focus of attention. It's used to being in charge, driving the bus, going where it wants, and keeping you busy with thinking, worrying, and planning. Just as you settle into the comfort of counting breaths, your mind will start sending distracting thoughts to get back in charge. Before you know it, you can be lost in thought and forget you were even counting.

Roadblock #2: Your Rebellious Body. Just like your mind, your body may not be used to sitting absolutely still and will do its best to distract you. As you sit in calm, some parts may twitch, tingle, or go numb. You might feel itchy, hungry, thirsty, achy . . . IF you allow yourself to focus on these sensations. Remember, the body and mind influence each other. All bodily distractions are really the expression of a restless mind. No matter how compelling a physical sensation may seem, it will go away if you cease to magnify it with your attention.

Roadblock #3: The World. Somehow the whole world seems to know when you're about to sit down to meditate. Friends stop by or your phone rings, people knock on your door, your little brother barges into the room, or the next-door neighbor picks this moment to mow the lawn.

Getting Around Roadblocks. If you are distracted by your mind, your body, or the world, return your attention to your breathing and focus on counting. Begin at "one" on the next inhalation and continue counting again. The first few times you try meditating, you may start over a lot. That's okay. With practice, you can improve your ability to stay focused on your breathing and detaching from your mind and body.

Progressive Muscle Relaxation (PMR)

When stressed people talk about being "uptight" or "tense," they're not just describing how they feel but also the condition of their muscles. In the 1920s, Dr. Edmund Jacobson learned that muscles could be deeply relaxed by intentionally holding and then releasing tension. Dr. Jacobson called this exercise Progressive Relaxation. Today it's referred to as Progressive Muscle Relaxation or PMR.

PMR is easy to do. You isolate different muscle groups, and systematically tighten and then release them. By developing a routine and practicing it regularly, you'll soon have another approach to finding your calm center.

One benefit of PMR is that you don't have to be alone in a quiet place to do it. You may want to learn in a safe and private setting, but once you become skilled at the technique, you can do it anytime or anywhere you like.

Getting Ready

- Wear comfortable clothing. Tight clothing or belts applying pressure to your body can cause you to be uncomfortable and make it difficult to concentrate. You may also wish to remove your shoes.

- Find a comfortable place to sit or lie down where it's quiet and you're not likely to be disturbed.

- While there is no risk of injury during PMR, be cautious about any muscles that have recently been injured or are prone to cramping.

- Take natural, relaxed breaths as you do the exercise, and keep your focus on what is happening in your muscles. Feel the buildup and release of tension in each particular muscle group. It is often helpful to visualize the particular muscle group being tensed and then released.

- When you are holding tension in one part of your body, make sure the other parts stay relaxed. Only tense the part you're training.

- As you go through the PMR exercise, it's important to notice the difference between tense and relaxed muscles.

Progressive Muscle Relaxation (PMR) Exercise

1. Begin your PMR session by tensing the muscles in your feet. Bend your toes down and hold them 3–5 seconds. You may want to count to yourself saying one thousand one, one thousand two . . . up to five. Then quickly release the tension. Next, pull your toes up and again hold that position as tight as you can for 3–5 seconds. Again, quickly relax your feet. Notice the sensation of release and the absence of tension.

2. Next, tighten all the muscles from your feet up to your waist. Start with tightening your calf muscles, then tighten your thighs, and finally squeeze your buttocks. Check to see that your feet and everything above your waist is relaxed.

Hold them all as tightly as you can for 3–5 seconds . . . and then quickly release. Again, take a moment to notice the sensation of release and how it feels to have the tension drain away.

3. Now repeat this procedure with the muscles in your stomach. Tighten and hold the tension for 3–5 seconds, and then release and pause to notice the feeling.

4. Moving up to your chest—tighten those muscles and hold the tension for 3–5 seconds . . . and then release. Release your breath.

5. Now tense the muscles in your shoulders by lifting and holding them for 3–5 seconds. Make sure to have all the surrounding muscles relaxed and keep the tension in the area of your shoulders. Then release the muscles in your shoulders and feel them sinking back on to the floor.

6. Tighten just your hands by forming fists. Hold them tightly for 3–5 seconds and release the effort and tension.

7. Tighten your hands by bending them back at the wrist. Continue to build the tension in your forearms, biceps, and triceps. Hold this position for 3–5 seconds and release and let the muscles soften and relax.

8. Tense your neck by turning your head as far as you can to the right and holding it for 3–5 seconds. Then turn your head back to center and relax. Now turn it to the left as far as you can and hold that position for 3–5 seconds. Again, return to center and release the effort. Feel the weight of your head on the floor.

9. Next contract the muscles in your face. Press your lips together, wrinkle your nose, tighten your forehead and squeeze your eyes shut. Hold this position for 3–5 seconds, and then quickly let the tension drain away and feel your face returning to it's normal position.

10. Finally, do a quick scan of your whole body for any remaining tension. Imagine a wave of relaxation starting at your toes, moving up your body, up your arms, and sweeping any remaining tension right out the top of your head. Enjoy the feeling of deep muscle relaxation and whole body calm.

11. When you're ready, take a couple of slow, deep breaths, open your eyes, put a smile on your face, then sit up and head back into your life . . . refreshed.

This may seem like a lot to do, but once you've been through it a few times, it goes fairly quickly. The whole activity, tensing and releasing each part of your body and pausing to feel the sensations of relaxation in between, can be done in 10–15 minutes. When you're finished, your body will feel very heavy and calm with the tension released. Your breathing and heart rate will have slowed down and your mind will be more likely to enter into a relaxed state. Learning PMR is great because it allows you to have greater awareness of your body and release tension in the moment you experience it.

Will relaxation skills completely eliminate stress from your life or make your wildest dreams come true? Probably not. But they can help you feel less overwhelmed, worried, or insecure. Real relaxation takes you directly to the calm place in the center of the stress storm and allows you to experience deep physical release and mental calm. The more you practice relaxation skills, the more capable you become of staying centered in calm—throughout a regular day as well as when you're surrounded by invisible tigers.

Find Out More

Breathe: Yoga for Teens by Mary Kaye Chryssicas. Filled with many full-color illustrations, this yoga instruction book features many positions and breathing techniques that can help you lessen tension and feel your best. A DVD also is included.

Indigo Teen Dreams by Lori Lite. This audiobook features breathing exercises, visualization prompts, muscle relaxation techniques, and other self-calming methods to reduce stress and feel good about yourself.

Teens Health (www.teenshealth.org). This Web site offers information on all kinds of issues that can stress you out and includes techniques you can use to slow down and relax.

"Problems come up with other people no matter what you say or do. It's all about knowing what to do when that happens."
—**Maria, 14**

"Sometimes I feel like I'm pushed around—not physically but by what others want. I'm just starting to speak up for myself when something isn't right for me."
—**Kevin, 15**

"I wish my parents trusted me more. I don't get to do half the stuff my friends do."
—**Tavaris, 13**

"I know school is important, but a lot of the time it feels like an exercise in people abuse."
—**Lori, 16**

Stand Up for Yourself

A lot of the stress we feel comes from how we get along with others. For example, at times, you may feel other people—including parents, teachers, or other adults—have too much control over your life. Maybe you sometimes feel like your needs, opinions, and feelings don't count, that everything is decided for you. Or maybe you feel like your family and school responsibilities take up a lot of your free time. And when you do have time for yourself, maybe limits are placed on what you can do or how much time you spend doing the activities you enjoy. Assertiveness skills can help you with the stress caused by these kinds of situations.

Assertiveness Skills

Others may have a lot to say about some parts of your life, but you actually have more control than you might realize. Some rules at school or home don't seem fair, but you probably know from experience that rebelling against them doesn't usually help. Assertiveness skills can help you stand up for yourself in positive ways.

Assertiveness Quiz

1. If teachers are unfair, do you talk to them about it?

2. If you know a friend lies to you, do you say something?

3. If a person sends nasty text messages about you, do you talk with someone about it?

4. If you're waiting in line and someone cuts in front of you, do you speak up?

5. Do you confront people who try to embarrass or gossip about you?

6. If a friend wants you to do something you're not comfortable with, can you say "no"?

7. Can you discuss family rules (like curfew or chores) without arguing?

8. If someone is bullying you at school, are you able to tell a teacher?

9. Are you able to tell your friends the truth about what you think and who you are?

10. Are you able to resolve conflicts with others without getting angry and aggressive?

If you answered no to some or most of these questions, you could benefit from a boost in assertiveness. Assertiveness skills help you honestly share your thoughts and feelings without disrespecting others. They help you set limits on what is and isn't okay with you and ask for what you want and need. When you're assertive, people know who you are and what you think and feel, and they understand your ground rules for relationships. Assertiveness can help you protect the rights you have as a person.

Your Basic Rights

- You have the right to have your feelings, needs, and opinions heard and considered.

- You have the right to have input into the decisions that affect your life.

- You have the right to say, "No," "I don't know," or "I don't understand."

- You have the right to stand up to people who threaten, tease, or put you down.

- You have the right to share your feelings.

- You have the right to like yourself even though you're not perfect.

- You have the right to respond to violations of your rights.

These rights also come with responsibilities. For example, you don't have the right to share your feelings about others by putting them down or physically hurting them—assertiveness is not the same as aggressiveness. Being aggressive doesn't consider others' feelings, costs you respect, and can drive people away. When you're assertive, on the other hand, you can handle challenges in ways that are respectful and recognize others' feelings.

The ASSERT Formula

You might know from experience that keeping a level head when you feel you've been wronged can be difficult. Tough situations can come up and make it hard to keep your cool. Other times you might feel afraid to speak up about something that's bothering you. Assertiveness skills come in handy in all of these situations.

ASSERT Formula

A—Attention
S—Soon, Simple, Short
S—Specific
E—Effect
R—Response
T—Terms

Attention. To work on problems you're having with others, you first have to get their **attention**. Engage the person in a respectful way and tell him or her you want to talk about something important.

Soon, Simple, Short. Respond as **soon** as possible to a situation. Letting something go unaddressed can cause you stress for a long time. If you're really upset and afraid you might react in a negative or harmful way, then talk to the person as soon as you've calmed down. When you are ready to discuss the issue, keep your explanation of the problem **simple** and **short**.

Specific. When you're describing the situation, focus on the **specific** behavior—what a person has said or done—that's causing you to be uncomfortable.

Effect. Help others understand the **effect** a situation is having on you. Share with the other person how the specific behavior causes you to feel.

Response. Describe the **response** you would like from him or her that would help resolve the issue. Then ask the other person for feedback on your request.

Terms. Finally, after discussing the specific behavior and your request for change, briefly re-state the **terms** of your mutual agreement to make sure everything is clear.

Here are three examples of how and when to use the ASSERT formula to give you an idea of what it will sound like when you put it into action:

Situation #1

There's a scuffle near you in the hall at school. Some teachers break it up and take away the students who were fighting. One of the teachers takes you to the office. You try to explain you weren't involved in the fight, but the teacher isn't listening.

Attention: "Mrs. Williams, can I talk to you about what just happened?"

Soon, Simple, Short: "I wasn't involved in the fight in any way, and I feel it's unfair for me to be punished."

Specific: "I understand that you thought I was involved, and I can see how you made the mistake. But I was only walking by when the fight began."

Effect: "I'm upset because I don't want to be suspended and miss school for something I didn't do. I also feel hurt that you believe I'd even think of fighting in school."

Response: "Would you be willing to listen to my side of the story? I was close to the situation and can tell you what I saw."

Terms: "Thanks. I really appreciate knowing that you're willing to hear me out."

Situation #2

Your mom yells at you to get off the phone when you're talking with friends. Your friends can hear her, and the shouting embarrasses you.

Attention: "Mom, can we take a second to talk about what just happened while I was on the phone? This is really important to me."

Soon, Simple, Short: "I'm having a problem with how you let me know when you want me to get off the phone."

Specific: "I don't like being yelled at when you feel I've been on the phone too long."

Effect on Me: "When you do that, my friends hear you and I'm embarrassed."

Response: "Would you be willing to try something different? If you held up two fingers to let me know I have two minutes to get off the phone, it would give me enough time to finish my conversation. I think it would be easier on both of us."

Terms: "Okay, so you'll hold up two fingers instead of yelling, and I'll get off the phone within two minutes. Thanks for being willing to try this idea."

Situation #3

A longtime friend from the neighborhood has joined the football team and now mostly hangs out with other players at school. If your friend sees you when he's with the team, he ignores you. You haven't hung out together in a few weeks.

Attention: "Hey, Jake. Do you have a minute to talk about something that's bothering me?"

Soon, Simple, Short: "Ever since you joined the football team, it seems like you don't have time for our friendship."

Specific: "It seems like you only spend time with other players, and when I do see you, you ignore me. We hardly hang out anymore."

Effect: "It's cool that you're on the football team, and I understand you need to have other friends. But I feel hurt because we've been close for a long time and now it seems like you don't want to spend time with me."

Response: "I would still like to hang out with you once in a while. Maybe we could get together at a time when you don't have practice."

Terms: "Thanks. I really appreciate knowing you still care about our friendship and that you want to spend time together. See you Sunday!"

(If Jake doesn't have time to hang out with you, it might be time to build other friendships. "Weave a Safety Net" on pages 67–75 has some ideas for expanding your social circle.)

The ASSERT formula may feel mechanical and awkward at first, but with practice it can become more natural. Even though it's a simple formula, it can be quite powerful. When you are assertive with others about what you want to happen, you are more likely to get your needs met as well as get more respect. While you may not always get what you want, at least you've explained how you feel and tried to make the situation better. Using this form of assertiveness is like saying, "I'm taking this risk because I care about our relationship and I want us both to be happy." That kind of statement can go a long way toward how people see and treat you in the future.

Expressing your feelings in positive and assertive ways is like having a safety valve that allows you to release the pressure of strong negative feelings and keeps you from reaching the bursting point. It can also help you understand yourself better, feel less vulnerable, and get more of what you want and deserve in life. That's much better than heading out into a jungle full of threatening stress tigers without any defenses.

Important!

It's important to use your judgment when using the ASSERT formula. For example, you don't want to provoke someone who is violent, abusive, or under the influence of drugs or alcohol. These skills work best when you're dealing with a person who is reasonable and ready and willing to hear your side of an issue. If you ever feel your safety is in danger, get away from the situation and find help right away.

Find Out More

Above the Influence (www.abovetheinfluence.com). A Web site from the U.S. government, Above the Influence is a resource for teens looking to move beyond peer pressure and stand up for their values and beliefs. The site features games, videos, quizzes, student stories, and suggestions for staying assertive when others try to make decisions for you.

Stick Up for Yourself! Every Kid's Guide to Personal Power and Positive Self-Esteem **by Gershen Kaufman, Lev Raphael, and Pamela Espeland.** This book provides real-life scenarios and personal power tools you can use to stand firm when others want to push you around. Find out what to say in tough situations, ideas for ending conflicts, and much more.

"I have a friend that would do anything to be there for me. She is my truest friend and I'd be lost without her."
—**Tabitha, 12**

"My family and friends are behind me 100%. They give me confidence and tell me if I'm messing up so that I can fix whatever's going on."
—**Wayne, 13**

"Life is nothing without family and friends to share it with."
—**Alexander, 15**

"I can go to my nana with any problem. When other people don't understand, it's her I can trust."
—**Rachel, 16**

Weave a Safety Net of Support

Have you ever felt stressed about something but kept the problem to yourself? Maybe you didn't want to worry anyone or you were afraid others would look down on you. It's natural to want to appear capable, strong, and able to get through tough times. But sometimes the fear of showing uncertainty or vulnerability can make us close ourselves off when we're most in need of support. It's during hard or stressful times that a safety net of trusted people can be especially helpful.

The Importance of Weaving a Safety Net

Sometimes it can feel like we're supposed to be superheroes—to handle all the challenges in life alone, and if we can't, then something is wrong with us. It also can seem like we should be able to do new things on our own, even if we've never done them before. Unfortunately, these thoughts have the power to make us feel bad about ourselves and think we're alone in dealing with the stressful parts of life.

- Do you feel the need to put up a front or try to impress others?

- Do you ever say you're doing fine—even when you're not feeling well?

- Do you feel like you have to sometimes lie about what you like or who you are?

- Do you wonder if you can really trust people for support when you're in a crisis?

- Do you feel you have to "go it alone" when you're overwhelmed, frightened, or confused?

Healing Friends

Friendship and family support are so important that they actually affect your physical health. Studies show that spending time and talking with caring friends and family members reduces the presence of cortisol and other stress hormones that delay healing. Connecting with others even has benefits at the cellular level!

The truth is, family and friends are important sources of help for staying on top of stress and dealing with challenges. Together, these people form a safety net, much like the net under high-wire performers at a circus. Knowing they are there for you can give you the courage to face problems and try new things. When you're out there taking a risk, teetering on the wire, it's great to know you're not alone and there's a group of trustworthy people who will catch you if you fall.

Human safety nets don't simply appear when you need them. Instead they have to be intentionally created and strengthened over time. You can start by being a supportive person yourself. Being there for friends or family members when they're down or need help allows you to build trust. When you show you can be counted on, others are more likely to be there for you.

The Five Levels of Relationships

Think for a moment about the people you know. Are there some people you really trust and go to for help if you need it—like family members or best friends? Are there others you know but aren't especially close to? If you think about it, you probably have all kinds of different relationships—from people you can't live without to people you find it hard to live with.

If you had to grade your relationships, you might start by thinking about how much you trust them. A trust scale might look like this:

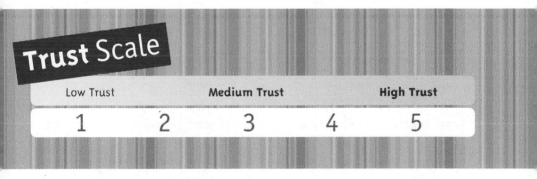

One way to gauge the amount of trust in a relationship is to think about the things you talk about with other people. What do you share with friends and family members? What do these people share with you? As you read the following descriptions, think about the people you know and which categories they might fit into.

Level 1—"Just the facts . . ."

In Level 1 relationships, facts are shared. A lot of everyday conversation between acquaintances is spent at Level 1. It's nonthreatening chat because it isn't about the people doing the talking.

"There's a basketball game on Saturday night."

"We're having a test on Chapter 4 this Friday."

"The weather is supposed to be good this weekend."

Level 2—"They say . . ."

Level 2 also is safe territory because conversations are about what other people have said. The risk is pretty low because you don't say what you are thinking or feeling. Instead, you're like a reporter sharing what you've heard, read, or seen somewhere else. Unfortunately, a lot of Level 2 talk can be gossip or put-downs toward others.

"I hear Debbie has a new boyfriend."

"They say the math teacher is tough."

"Paulo told me the team had an awful game last night."

Level 3—"I think . . ."

Level 3 conversations are where connections between people begin. Some trust is required at this level because you are taking a risk by revealing your opinions and ideas. There's the possibility of disagreement, but also the opportunity to build friendships based on things you share.

"That song is awesome."

"I think using drugs is stupid."

"We should have a say in how our school is run."

Level 4—"I feel . . ."

In Level 4 conversations, feelings are shared and genuine emotions are expressed. For example, a friend upset about a breakup wouldn't be afraid to cry or show feelings in front of you. At the same time, you would try to understand your friend's feelings and provide comfort. Level 4 conversations require trust because people can feel vulnerable and need to be confident of your support before opening up. This is the level where real connection between people takes place and solid friendships are formed.

> "My parents are getting divorced. I feel afraid and angry that they'd break up our family."

> "It makes me happy that my mom got the job she's always wanted."

> "I'm so upset about my grade on the math test that I could scream."

Level 5—"This is how I feel about you."

Level 5 is an extension of Level 4. At this level, you directly share your feelings for or about another person. This includes feelings of love, hurt, frustration, happiness, or whatever else is going on between you. While these conversations can be hard, they also can make relationships stronger. Think of a time when you and a parent argued but talked things over and came to an agreement. It's possible you felt closer after working things out. Level 5 relationships involve the greatest risk and require the most trust.

> "I appreciate how you stood up for me when Becca was putting me down. You really are a good friend, and I feel lucky to know you."

> "It makes me sad that you're moving. I don't want to lose your friendship."

> "I'm worried because you've seemed depressed for days, and the way you're acting scares me."

Here's what happens when we add this new information to the Trust Scale:

Now that you're familiar with the Trust Scale and the five levels of retionships, you can rate your own support system. Include family members, neighbors, friends, teachers, counselors, and other people at school or in your community.

Trust Scale

Low Trust		Medium Trust		High Trust
1	2	3	4	5
Just the facts . . .	They say . . .	I think . . .	I feel . . .	I feel . . . about us.
Randy	Abigail	LaTisha	Ken	Dad
Erin	Nora	Mr. Jacobsen	Ms. Lee	Mom
Brittany	Claudia	Mrs. Sampson	Rabbi Green	McKenzie
Aman	Kirsten	Will	Maria	Aunt Sally
Ai	Mary			Nana
Santana	Alex			

When you're done, you'll have a basic map of your relationships. You may have many 1s, 2s, and 3s but need to build some stronger 4 or 5 connections. Or you might have a couple of people you're really close to and that's about all. Whatever it looks like now, the map can tell you about the quality of your current safety net and help you identify relationships you'd like to make stronger.

Your goal doesn't have to be to turn all of your relationships into 5s—everyone also needs 1s, 2s, 3s, and 4s in their lives. These are people who can be fun to hang out with, teach you cool things, offer different perspectives, and introduce you to new experiences. While it's not essential to be extremely close with everyone you know, weaving a strong safety net does mean developing a few 4s and 5s in your life for support when you need it. Knowing you have people you can trust and count on keeps you from facing the invisible tigers of life on your own.

Strengthening Relationships

What can you do if you want to make your relationships with friends, family, and others stronger? Do you go up to someone and say: "Hey, we're about a 2 on the relationship scale. I'd like to see us reach level 4 or 5—do you want to discuss your deep feelings with me?" You could say this, but there's a good chance the other person would look at you like you're crazy—and then maybe run away. The good news: You can try many other less-awkward ways to strengthen relationships.

1. **Spend time together.** This may sound obvious, but activities with friends and family provide some of the best bonding experiences. No matter what you're doing, interesting or funny things are likely to happen that give you something to talk or laugh about together. Joining sports, drama, band, or other extra-curricular activities also are great ways to connect with others. As you spend time together and share interests, you'll have experiences that can bring you closer.

2. **Be honest.** When it comes to improving relationships, honesty is always the best policy. Lying to parents, teachers, or other adults results in distrust that damages relationships. The same is true for friendships. Lying to or about others is irresponsible and disrespectful. It can cause fallouts that are difficult to repair. The next time you feel the need to stretch the truth, remember that lies nearly always come back to hurt (or even destroy) relationships.

3. **Take an interest in things that are important to others.** Asking friends and family members about what they like can make them feel good because it shows you care about them. Most people enjoy talking about the activities in their lives, and the good feeling they have discussing these things can rub off on you.

4. **Don't pressure others.** Bossy people generally don't make very good friends. Do you want to hang around someone who constantly tells you what to do or tries to make you do things that you're uncomfortable with? Probably not. If you feel the urge to pressure someone or tell him or her what to do or think, try to stop yourself by remembering how it would feel coming back at you. Real friends give each other permission to be themselves.

5. Avoid overemphasizing yourself. It's good to share information about yourself with others—talking about your thoughts, feelings, and interests is a good way to establish common ground. At the same time, sharing can be overdone. You might know a few people who think the world revolves around them, they're doing the best things, and you're dying to hear all about their lives. Braggarts or "center of the universe" people usually do a pretty good job of turning others off. It's good to share, but it's also important to listen to what others have to say. In good friendships most aspects of the relationship are shared equally.

6. Offer your help. When you think someone could use a hand, offer it. Whether it's pitching in on chores at home or taking time to explain a math assignment to a classmate, make your move. Good deeds usually generate gratitude and good feelings—it's hard for people not to like someone who wants to help. The same holds true for difficult situations where you know even a quick chat or word of encouragement could do someone a world of good. You may not even be that close, but a gesture that says you understand how he or she is feeling shows your potential to become a close friend.

Find Out More

How Rude! The Teenagers' Guide to Good Manners, Proper Behavior, and Not Grossing People Out by Alex J. Packer. Getting along with others begins with politeness. This book has the lowdown on giving and getting respect.

The InSite (www.theinsite.org). Visit this site for information on dealing with the ups and downs of relationships—including friendship troubles, family spats, and rough spots with teachers and other adults.

Teen Central (www.teencentral.net). Teen Central features real stories about relationships and other issues. You also can submit your own questions and get feedback on them from others.

"I know where I'm going—even in the hard times I keep my eyes on the prize."
—**Ming, 15**

"Life is so much easier when you have an idea of what's going to happen next."
—**Asha, 17**

"If you don't make sure you're on the right path, who will?"
—**Ronald, 13**

"Goals give you more power over your own destiny."
—**Ingrid, 14**

Take Charge of Your Life

Do you ever feel like you're not in charge of your life? That you're doing the best you can but things just happen to you without your control? Maybe you feel so stressed out that right now all you can do is keep up, let alone think about what you want to do in the future. Feeling this way can make it seem like your life is a movie—one where you're only a character following directions from someone else calling the shots.

Not feeling in control of the action or being confused about how your movie should play out can cause a lot of stress. If you're not moving toward what you want, goals can help you get back in the director's chair. It is your life after all—why not make it great?

Writing Your Own Script

How can you get back in the director's chair? Ask yourself some important, big questions, the ones that have the power to shape your future: "Where is my life heading? Why am I going in this direction? Who decided? What's really important to me? What do I want be working toward?" These life questions can be difficult to answer—so difficult that many people avoid thinking about them at all. But charging through life without a sense of direction or purpose can leave you feeling like you're running in place. You can start taking charge by writing a script for a movie called *My Life*.

To start writing your script, think about the things you would like to accomplish. These might be goals you have for the immediate future (such as making the swim team) or longer-term achievements you'd like to work toward (like getting a college scholarship). No matter how big or small accomplishments might seem, setting goals helps you achieve them. And, you can reduce stress because you're working toward where you want to be.

Goal Questions

If you're having trouble coming up with goals, use these questions to get you thinking in the right direction.

1. **What are your interests or special talents?** People are happiest when they're doing what they really love or are good at. Try to imagine goals related to your interests, passions, and abilities.

2. **What would you most like to be known for?** When we're respected for our accomplishments, we're more likely to be happy. Think of achievements you might like to be known for.

3. **What's most important to you?** Doing things that are personally meaningful help us feel balanced and satisfied. Think of goals that would make you feel good about yourself.

4. **Who are your heroes?** The people we admire offer us a window into our own dreams. Think of your heroes—people you look up to who have made a difference in the world—and why they stand out to you. In what ways would you like their strengths and accomplishments to be reflected in yours?

5. **Where do you want to live?** Where we live can play a big role in the opportunities available to us. Try to imagine your dream location and how that might influence your goals for the future.

6. **If you could do absolutely anything with your life, what would you do?** Don't let anything limit your dreaming. If you had all the freedom, time, money, and support you needed, what would you love to do? Open up your imagination and see what comes out.

Answering these questions might help you set goals for the immediate future or long-term aspirations. Whatever the case, working toward them can help you feel good about yourself and less anxious about the future. You might even discover some strong themes that hint at what you want the movie of your life to be all about.

Reaching Your Goals

"I happen to have a lot of rhythm—something I was born with, I guess. I see a gig in a hip-hop act in my future . . . maybe even a recording contract."
—**Jakob, 14**

"I have a way with words, writing poetry and stories mostly. For me, writing is like breathing—I need to do it to go on living."
—**Brook, 13**

"I look up to doctors, nurses, first responders, police—basically anyone who goes out of their way to help others. It's important to me that I make that kind of difference."
—Samantha, 15

"Life on Earth is not for me—not because I don't like it here but because I'm into space travel. In 10 years I want to be living on the International Space Station."
—Bjorn, 14

"I'm really worried about the global climate. In my environmental studies course I'm learning a lot about climate change. I think that someday I'll do something to make a big difference for the planet."
—Ricardo, 16

Setting goals is important, but it's only a first step. You still need a plan to get to where you want to go. You can do this by setting up a series of short-term goals that support the accomplishments you have in mind. When you do this, you're breaking down big challenges into smaller, manageable chunks. Feature films may be impressive when they're all finished and up on the big screen, but they have to be shot one scene at a time.

Five-Step Goal Setting Plan

1. **Write a goal statement.** First and foremost, defining your goal is important. It's hard to accomplish something if you aren't clear about what it is you're trying to do. Be as specific as possible in describing what you want.

2. **Make a list of steps that lead to your goal.** Think about your overall objective and the things you need to do to reach it. These should be small steps that you can comfortably work on without causing stress. (If short-term goals seem impossible or intimidating, you may get frustrated and give up on them.) Keep breaking down goals until they are small enough to be easily accomplished.

3. **List some of the roadblocks you might encounter—and ideas for getting around them.** A lot of people give up on goals when they experience a snag in their plans and just go back to living in the moment. A good way to keep your forward momentum is by anticipating possible problems and coming up with solutions to them before they occur.

The Power of Goal Setting

Writing out your goals may seem like a lot of work, but it's also extremely powerful. Research shows that people who define goals are much more successful in working toward them. The mind is a powerful force, and when you direct it toward the things you want, you have a decisive advantage.

4. **List some of the resources that might be helpful toward achieving your goal.** Who can offer insight that will be helpful as you move forward? Are there books or Web sites that might be good resources? How about local or national organizations with special expertise on a topic? Think of all the different places where you might get information and support.

5. **List the ways you will measure progress toward your goal.** It's important to track the progress you're making as you go. If you don't pay attention to this step, it's possible to get offtrack and do a lot of work that doesn't help—and can even hurt—your efforts. And seeing your progress also can be motivating and give you confidence as you move forward.

Now that you know how goal setting works, let's put it into action to see how it might work in the real world. You can use this same process to outline a plan for reaching something you'd like to accomplish.

Reaching Your Goals

1. **Write a goal statement.**

   I'd like to get into a college or university program where I can study Web site development. During my last year of high school, I will improve my qualifications by getting real-world computer experience.

2. **Make a list of steps that lead to your goal.**

   I will:

   A. Secure an internship with a local tech company.

   B. Help maintain the school's Web site.

   C. Volunteer with a community education program that teaches technology skills to people with limited computer access.

   D. Join a computer club and work on collaborative Web projects.

   E. Create my own Web site that can serve as a portfolio of my skills.

3. **Write down some of the potential roadblocks you might encounter—and ideas for getting around them.**

   What might happen:

   A. There aren't any internship opportunities near me.

   What I can do: Get involved in a technology mentorship program or see if I can job shadow Joe's mom in her work as a Web designer.

B. My school doesn't have a computer club or a Web site.

What I can do: Start a computer club and volunteer to work on a new Web site for the school.

C. I don't know enough about building Web sites to create my own.

What I can do: Get help from the computer teacher Mr. Schmidt with the Web development skills I don't have.

4. **List some of the resources that might be helpful toward achieving your goal.**

A. Mr. Schmidt in the computer lab.

B. Manny, the kid who loves being called a computer geek.

C. Ms. Hannover, the guidance counselor.

D. Magazines about the computer industry.

E. People in the technology programs at the local community college.

5. **Write how you will measure progress toward your goal.**

A. I'm getting training and experience from an internship or mentor programs.

B. I'm working on the school's Web site.

C. I'm teaching others technology skills as I'm improving my own.

D. I'm involved in the computer club.

E. I'm building my own Web site (and it looks great!).

Going through this process with each of your goals takes time. But unless you make specific plans, the movie of your life may never be anything more than a daydream—one you at some point wake from and realize you're not where you want to be.

As you work toward goals, remember that the movie of your life is a work in progress. You should feel free to tweak the script and work on goals as your feelings or priorities change. You may want to keep your vision statement and goals in a computer document so you can make changes over time. It's also good to keep in mind that goal setting isn't just for your big life dreams. Use the same five-step goal setting process for the everyday stuff—big and small—to help you get the important things done and reduce stress in your life.

When you know and like where you're going, you'll feel less anxious and more at peace with yourself. You will also feel more in charge of your life and experience the joy, satisfaction, and self-confidence that come from turning your dreams into reality. You'll be working at making your life a mega successful feature film—one in which you are proud to have the starring role.

Find Out More

A Taste-Berry Teen's Guide to Setting and Achieving Goals **by Bettie and Jennifer Youngs.** Featuring the writing of dozens of teens, this book provides insight into goal setting as well as inspiration for those tough times when sticking with a plan can be hard.

Teens Can Make It Happen: Nine Steps to Success **by Stedman Graham.** This book features a nine-step plan to work toward long-term life goals by breaking down challenges into small, manageable tasks.

What Do You Really Want? How to Set a Goal and Go for It! **by Beverly K. Bachel.** With an inspiring foreword by polar explorer Ann Bancroft, this step-by-step book features advice on defining and accomplishing goals.

"My schedule's like one of those arrival/departure boards at the airport—packed. If I'm not careful with my time I fall behind fast."
—**Brooke, 14**

"Time seems to go faster and faster. I don't know if it actually does or if jamming more things into my day just makes it seem that way."
—**Will, 16**

"Getting stuff done is important—and knowing how to manage my time helps me do that."
—**Ahn, 13**

"It's tough to know where to draw the line when you're figuring out what you can or can't do to help someone."
—**Eric, 15**

#7

Get Time on Your Side

Say it's Sunday morning and you open your eyes to a blue sky. You imagine going to the beach for some fun and then you remember all the things you have to do: Your dad's been asking you to help in the garden. It's also your mom's birthday next week and you haven't picked up a card or cake mix. Then there's your schoolwork—a huge history test on Monday and an English paper due Friday. You also should be preparing for the internship interview you have on Wednesday. Oh, and you'd like to replace your favorite CD, which the dog seems to have mistaken for a chew toy. Other than that, you don't have much going on!

Does it seem possible to get all of this done? Does life feel like an ongoing collection of things to do and you're never caught up? Does it seem like there's not enough time to do all of the stuff you have to do, let alone free time for doing other things you enjoy? If you're feeling the pressure of a lot of got-tos, here's a stress-fighting skill that can help: time management.

How Time Management Can Help You

A busy schedule can make it very difficult to get everything done. You can become your own worst invisible tiger by over-scheduling and putting too much pressure on yourself. To keep this from happening, use time management skills. These tools can help you stay on top of tasks and make decisions about your schedule, no matter how busy you might be.

Get Your Sleep

If you think skipping sleep is the solution to your time shortage, think again. Experts recommend nine to ten hours of sleep each night for teens—any fewer and you can experience less energy, more stress, poor concentration, and even feelings of sadness or depression. A big part of sleep deprivation is having too much to do—after a full day of school, sports, drama, a job, or other activities, you might not be able to think about homework until it's already late. Another factor: Researchers are finding out what a lot of teens already know—it's often hard for teens to fall asleep until late at night. A teen's biological clock shifts sleep cycles to later hours and makes going to bed early a huge challenge. Lack of a full night of rest can have you sleepwalking through life with invisible stress tigers stalking your every step.

Setting Priorities

One thing time management tools help you do is decide what's important to get done now and what you can do later. Prioritizing tasks and being clear about which things are most important can help you feel more in control of your life and get rid of the stressful feeling that everything needs to be done right now. Try the "ABC" method, a simple system of prioritization, to bring some order out of the chaos of too much to do.

The ABC Method

1. **Start by making a to-do list of all the things you need to get done in the near future.** Include items with firm deadlines (like assignments) as well as regularly occurring events that happen throughout the week—things like spending time with family and friends, shopping, exercise, chores, and anything else you have going on.

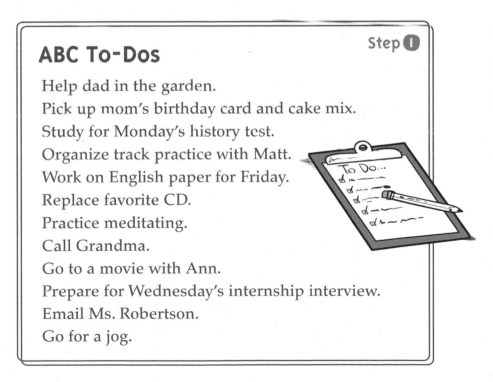

ABC To-Dos

Step ❶

Help dad in the garden.
Pick up mom's birthday card and cake mix.
Study for Monday's history test.
Organize track practice with Matt.
Work on English paper for Friday.
Replace favorite CD.
Practice meditating.
Call Grandma.
Go to a movie with Ann.
Prepare for Wednesday's internship interview.
Email Ms. Robertson.
Go for a jog.

2. **Now rank each item on your list according to this scale:**
   A—Very important and needs to be done as soon as possible.
   B—Pretty important, but can wait until A's are finished.
   C—Nice to do, but not essential.

   Let's say, for example, Sunday is the only day to work in the garden with your dad. This makes it a high-priority item—an "A." Working on your English paper is important, but it's not due right away—you could make it a "B." You really like Ann and going to the movie with her would be fun, but it's probably a "C," because it isn't essential to go right away. When you get done, your list might look something like this:

ABC To-Dos   Step ❷

A. Help dad in the garden.

B. Pick up mom's birthday card and cake mix.

A. Study for Monday's history test.

C. Organize track practice with Matt.

B. Work on English paper for Friday.

C. Replace favorite CD.

B. Practice meditating.

B. Call Grandma.

C. Go to a movie with Ann.

A. Prepare for Wednesday's internship interview.

A. Email Ms. Robertson.

C. Go for a jog.

---

3. **Now group all the A's, B's, and C's together.** Once you have them grouped, rank the items in each group individually (since you have several of each). The most important A should be given an A-1 ranking, the next most important A-2, and so on through your list. The last step is to put each group in numerical order. The result would look something like this:

ABC To-Dos   Step ❸

A-1. Help dad in the garden.

A-2. Study for Monday's history test.

A-3. Email Ms. Robertson.

A-4. Prepare for Wednesday's internship interview.

B-1. Pick up mom's birthday card and cake mix.

B-2. Work on English paper for Friday.

B-3. Call Grandma.

B-4. Practice meditating.

C-1. Organize track practice with Matt.

C-2. Go for a jog.

C-3. Go to a movie with Ann.

C-4. Replace favorite CD.

You are much clearer about which items are top priorities and which can wait. When you finish with the A's, you move onto the B's, and then, if you have time, move on to the C's. If you really don't have time to "do it all" after you prioritize your to-dos, you'll at

least know that the important things aren't falling though the cracks. You'll also be able to see which activities you can worry less about or eliminate altogether.

Your prioritized list isn't carved in stone, so your challenges may change from one day to the next or, sometimes, from one hour to the next. For example, the due date on your English paper might get pushed back a week, or your friend Ann doesn't have time to see a movie until next weekend. When changes happen, adjust your list of priorities accordingly. What task you tackle next also will depend on what time it is. For example, if it's later in the evening, getting a card and cake mix for your mom's birthday might not be possible. It might be just the right time, however, to do your meditation exercise.

Your goal is not to accomplish everything on your list. If that's how things work out, great, but don't push yourself too hard. Just do the best you can in the time you've got. At least you'll be getting the important things done, and knowing that can relieve a lot of stress.

If you don't prioritize your time, you can be left with a large collection of to-dos and a "do-everything-now-or-else" mentality. Everything seems to demand your attention, which almost guarantees every day will be full of stress and panic. The rest of this section includes more time management strategies to help make you an expert tiger tamer.

Time Management Tips

1. **Give yourself the freedom to say no.** People can quickly become overwhelmed when they try to please others and can't say no—whether it's chatting online, helping someone with a project, or just hanging out. It's important to know your limits and turn down invitations when you don't have time. If you feel overbooked, and barely have time for the A's on your prioritization list, it's time to start saying "no" to requests for your time. Also look at the activities toward the bottom of your list for opportunities to free up your schedule. Learning to say "no" shows self-respect and helps you focus on what's important to you.

2. **Know when you're at your best.** You can make the best use of time by knowing when you do things well. Some people study best in the early mornings and like to be active in the afternoons. Others like a quiet house later at night for homework and getting as much sleep as possible in the morning. If you know when you're at your best for a given task, try to structure that time in your life . . . and then resist phone calls, texts, emails, and other distractions. When you are following a similar plan each day, you can be more efficient at getting tasks done.

3. **Get your rest.** Sleeping might not seem like a way to get things done, but solid rest can help you feel refreshed and ready to take on the day's challenges. When you get enough sleep, your mind is more alert and can perform at its highest level. Your body also will have rested, which keeps you from feeling tired or sluggish.

4. Schedule breaks. Time management is not about doing something every possible second. Breaks are an important part of staying alert and productive. If you've been hard at work on a paper for a long time, take time to get up, stretch your muscles, and maybe get a snack. A little exercise, like a short walk, is a good way to regain focus. Listening to music or playing with the dog are great for short breaks as long as they don't become giant distractions.

5. Beware of time wasters. It's okay to spend some time playing video games, going online, connecting with a friend, or watching TV, but be careful about going overboard. These activities can suck you in for hours at a time. You might innocently flip on the TV or start playing a computer game during a break and not realize how much time is passing—the next thing you know it's midnight, you're tired, and you don't have your work done.

6. Use a calendar or planner. You may use an assignment notebook or another scheduling tool at school, but do you have something for tracking other events—like extracurricular activities, social commitments, or family events? A planner lets you see your schedule laid out and know what's ahead so you don't over-commit. You can create a planner using an ordinary notebook, or most mobile phones and email programs have scheduling tools you can use to stay on top of tasks.

When you prioritize and manage your time, you can create order out of stress-filled chaos. Taking charge of your life can give you a sense of accomplishment and build self-esteem. It also helps you stay on top of invisible tigers and make time for something else that's very important—rest and relaxation.

Find Out More

Don't Sweat the Small Stuff for Teens: Simple Ways to Keep Your Cool in Stressful Times by **Richard Carlson.** Including stories of real teens taking on stressful times, *Don't Sweat the Small Stuff for Teens* has practical strategies for evaluating what's important to you and using your time and energy for the important things in life.

The 7 Habits of Highly Effective Teens by **Sean Covey.** This book features time management tips as well as advice on big-picture life issues. Action plans can help you set priorities and overcome obstacles.

"I'm proud of stuff I've done, but I'm more excited about what the future holds."
—**Caryn, 16**

"I worry I'm going to make mistakes whenever I'm trying something for the first time. I'd like to feel less afraid."
—**Terrance, 15**

"Life is most exciting when I'm trying new things."
—**Zeek, 12**

"If I'm not challenging myself, I feel like I'm running in place."
—**Britt, 13**

Risk Trying New Things

What do you think of when you hear "take a risk"? If you're like many people, you might think of risk taking as bad, something that can only lead to trouble. While some risks definitely are bad (like using drugs or doing dangerous stunts), positive risk taking is an important skill that can improve your life and reduce stress. How? Taking risks enables you to explore your interests, learn new things, and face difficult challenges. Rather than easing along comfortably, you can push your limits to see what you're capable of.

Are You a Risk Taker?

Here are a few questions to help you decide if you're a risk taker. Which of the following would you rather do?

- Hang out with your usual friends or introduce yourself to new people?

- Take a course you know is easy or a more interesting one that will be challenging?

- Stick with the same activities after school or try something new?

If you're like many people, the first options probably seem more attractive because they're easy and comfortable. Trying something different can be intimidating. That's because you're taking a risk—a risk that new people won't like you, that you won't do well in a class, that you won't do something well on your first try.

Putting yourself on the line takes courage. You may not know exactly what you're in for, and your current level of knowledge and experience might not be enough to get you through. It's natural to feel uncertain and have a lot of Whatifs ("What if I make a fool of myself onstage?") and Wouldbuts ("I would try out for the team but I've never played organized sports before"). But choosing not to do something won't enable you to change or grow into your full potential.

The Amazing Brain

Did you know the human brain is elastic? The brain is made up of billions of neurons that change and adapt when faced with new questions or challenges. Researchers know this from brain scans, which show areas of focused neuron activity in the prefrontal cortex when people are engaged in learning. What does this mean? With study of a subject or practice of a skill, new neural pathways are formed that enable us to be more knowledgeable and efficient at tasks. For example, learning a new language: As the brain is exercised through study and practice, it becomes better at recalling vocabulary. When we push ourselves, we learn and grow.

Start Small and Give Yourself a Chance to Learn

When taking a risk, you don't have to focus on the final outcome right away. Instead, go for the next small step you might take. For example, if you decide that you want to run a marathon, you might not succeed if the race were tomorrow. Marathons are 26.2 miles, that's a long distance even for experienced runners. It doesn't make much sense to enter that race without a lot of preparation. But you can start small—maybe by talking with a coach at school about what goes into running a marathon and setting up a training program to gradually build your endurance. As you prepare and understand more about a challenge, you'll be more ready to take the next step . . . and then the next . . . and the next until you're crossing the finish line.

The point: Small steps are important toward taking risks or trying new things. Continually reaching small milestones keeps you motivated, and the progress you make can give you confidence for meeting future challenges.

Avoiding Perfectionism

Risk taking can be tough for people who believe they have to succeed right away and be good at everything they do. This is called perfectionism, and it's hard on people because their self-esteem is on the line every minute—which is stressful. Often these people push themselves in all areas of life.

Because it's humanly impossible to be perfect, perfectionism is a guaranteed prescription for feeling like you're not good enough. Many people with perfectionism start to experience depression or hopelessness because they can't live up to their own extreme expectations.

Because perfectionism keeps people from taking risks or trying new things, it is a huge barrier to growing and changing. It also can cause people to slow down. For example, a perfectionist might do the same assignment over and over to make it just right—even though it was done well the first time. While we can all be a little perfectionistic at times, for some people, it affects every part of their lives. To find out how much perfectionism affects you, take the following quiz. Read each statement and decide how much or how little you agree with it using the number system. You can write numbers on a separate sheet of paper—you'll add them up at the end.

Are You a Perfectionist?

Rating Scale
+2 = Strongly agree.
+1 = Somewhat agree.
 0 = No feeling.
-1 = Slightly disagree.
-2 = Strongly disagree.

1. If I don't set the highest standards for myself, I'll be a failure.

2. People will think less of me if I make mistakes.

3. If I can't do something really well, there's no point in doing it.

4. I get upset if I make a mistake.

5. If I try hard enough, I should be able to excel at anything.

6. It's immature to display any weakness.

7. I shouldn't have to repeat the same mistake more than once.

8. Being average at something isn't satisfying or worthwhile.

9. Failing makes me less of a person.

10. Getting upset about mistakes will help me do better next time.

Five Ways to Fight Perfectionism

When you're done answering the questions, total your score. A score above zero suggests some perfectionistic tendencies. If you have a very high score (like 15–20), life is probably pretty stressful for you. It's important to talk with a parent, counselor, or another trusted adult if you feel this kind of pressure. Here are five ways to fight perfectionism.

1. **Give yourself permission to make mistakes.** Remind yourself that you don't have to be absolutely perfect, we're all human, and it's okay to make mistakes. When you're working on something, think, "I know I may not do this perfectly but that's okay. Mistakes can help me learn, and doing my best is good enough." Keep repeating this thought as you work.

2. **Set limits on your time.** Do you ever spend too much time trying to do something perfectly? Maybe you have the feeling that no matter how much effort you put into a project, you have to continue working to improve it. To help stop this, think about how long something should take before you start it. Work on the project until you've spent that amount of time, and then stop. If you feel you need to spend more time on something, you can check in with a teacher for an objective opinion on your progress.

3. **Talk yourself out of negative thinking.** Reduce your negative thoughts by using positive self-talk. One way to do this is to outnumber bad thoughts with good ones. For every negative thought that enters your mind, think of five positive ones. You can learn more about positive self-talk on page 117.

4. **Address perfectionism in your family.** Often teens "inherit" their perfectionistic traits from parents or other family members. Maybe adults around you are perfectionists, and you've learned the behavior. Or perhaps you feel like the people around you expect your performance in school or other activities to be perfect. If this is true, it's important to talk with an adult you trust—someone not pressuring you—to get perspective on the situation and ideas for bringing up the subject with those you live with.

5. **Give yourself a break.** It's natural to want to do your best at school and in other activities. But it's also important to do some things that are just for fun. Put yourself in situations where you're not worried about how well you're doing, but instead are simply enjoying an activity. Take a walk, watch a movie, throw a frisbee, call a family member, or anything else that you enjoy doing.

Good or Bad Risk?

How can you tell if a risk is good or bad? Think of the worst possible outcome. Will your or anyone else's safety be in danger? Will property be destroyed? Is it illegal? Will anyone's feelings be hurt? If the answer is yes to any of these questions, it's a bad risk. If the worst thing that could happen is a little embarrassment, the risk is probably one you can take. For more on measuring risks, see "Stand on Solid Ground" (pages 107–113).

20 Positive Ways to Challenge Yourself

1. form a club
2. make new friends
3. run for student government
4. report stories for newspaper, radio, or television
5. speak up in class
6. take challenging courses
7. stand up for yourself
8. join the school play
9. build your own Web site
10. start a blog
11. enter a talent contest
12. try out for a team
13. form a music group
14. display your drawings, paintings, or photographs
15. volunteer with a neighborhood organization
16. make your own comic book
17. share your creative writing with others
18. take cooking classes
19. become a mentor
20. join the school band

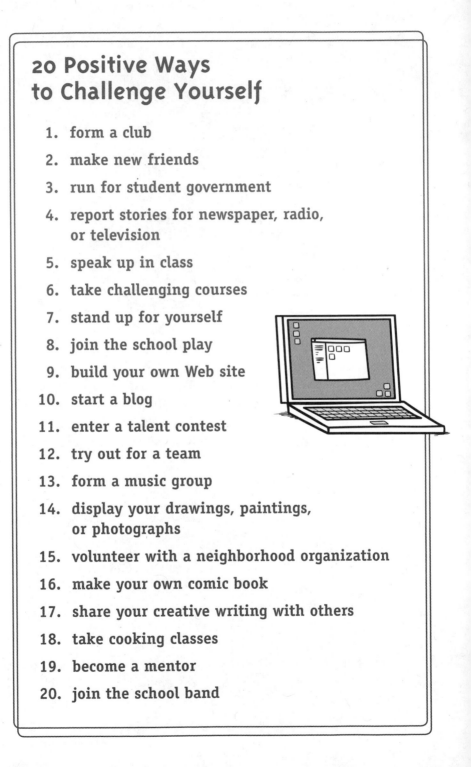

Find Support and Celebrate Successes

Taking risks doesn't mean going it alone with no help from others. In fact, it's important to get encouragement and advice from people. Parents, friends, neighbors, members of the community, professionals working in a certain field, and others you trust can help if you encounter any obstacles. There may still be times when things don't work out the way you plan, but these people can help you get back on track. Risk taking and support go hand in hand.

It's also important to celebrate your successes, even if they seem small. Big achievements don't usually happen overnight. Instead, they are the result of smaller accomplishments over a longer period of time. Steps you complete in areas that are new to you deserve to be acknowledged and celebrated—they're proof of your progress toward your goals and they're great motivators. You might even design a reward system for your accomplishments by doing nice things for yourself at steps along the way.

Find Out More

Mentor/National Mentoring Project (www.mentor.org). Looking for people to support you in life? Log on to this Web site to learn about mentoring agencies in your community.

Perfectionism: What's Bad About Being Too Good? **by Miriam Adderholdt and Jan Goldberg.** If you struggle with perfectionism, this book can help. It offers strategies that can help you get out of the mindset of thinking everything has to be done perfectly or extremely well.

"My friends push me a lot, even when I say I don't want to do something. It can be hard to be yourself and be accepted at the same time."
—**Jonah, 14**

"I like the feeling I get when I make decisions I know are right for me. My really good friends are going to like me regardless of my choices."
—**Sharon, 13**

"If I don't like a situation, I leave. It's as simple as that."
—**Dominic, 15**

"I used to get mad very easily and do things that made situations worse. Now I think about what I'm going to do before I act."
—**Olivia, 16**

#9

Stand on Solid Ground

Can you imagine what it would be like to experience an earthquake with everything around you in motion—buildings teetering back and forth, the pavement under your feet shifting up, down, sideways? Now imagine living that way for a long time, the earth constantly moving under your feet, always feeling anxious and unsure of what you should do next. Not knowing what decisions to make during stressful times can feel a lot like standing on shaky ground. Decision-making skills can help you feel in control again and reduce the amount of stress you feel.

Decisions Are Powerful

Most of life comes down to the decisions you make. What you decide to do helps determine whether good or bad things will happen. When you were younger, your family and other people made a lot of decisions for you. While you probably still get guidance from adults and have rules to follow, getting older means making more of your own choices. But with these new freedoms also comes more responsibility. That's why it's important to remember the bottom line on decisions—every single one matters. It's not always easy to know what decision to make—especially when you might be feeling pressure from someone.

Good or Bad Decision?

1. Will anyone be put in danger?

2. Will anyone be disrespected or insulted?

3. Will anyone's property be stolen or damaged?

4. Will this decision make a situation worse?

5. Will I be breaking any laws?

6. Will I have to lie about something?

7. Will I be escalating a conflict?

8. Will I get in trouble with my parents, my school, or the law?

9. Will I be letting people down?

10. Will I feel bad about myself afterward?

Unless you can absolutely, positively answer no to each question, you should seriously consider whether your decision is a good one. It's also a good idea to get the advice of a parent, counselor, or another adult when making a big decision.

Making Decisions When the Pressure's On

A lot of things can get in the way of making a good decision—including strong feelings. Anger and other powerful emotions can cause us to react in destructive ways when we're in a tough situation. Often when we lose control and act without thinking, we can resort to using violence, swearing, yelling, making threats, using put-downs, breaking things, or defying authority figures.

What can you do to keep a clear head when someone's really pushing you or you feel like you might lose control?

10 Tips for Tough Situations

1. **Step out.** Just for a moment, step out of the situation, take a few deep breaths, and try to collect your thoughts. Count down from 10, promising yourself you won't do or say anything until you reach zero.

2. **Consider options.** List three options for yourself . . . three different ways in which you could address the situation. Having a few choices increases the likelihood you'll make the best decision in the moment. If you have time, it's always good to talk with others you trust to get perspective and help coming up with solutions to problems.

3. **Visualize consequences.** Think about the possible consequences of your decision—what's the absolute worst thing that could result from responding in the wrong way? Will someone be hurt? Will you get in trouble? Imagine yourself in the situation—what will it feel like for you or how will people react?

4. *Retaliation makes things worse.* If your behavior is a reaction out of anger to what someone said or did, it's likely you won't make a good decision. Just because someone did something foolish does not give you a free pass to get revenge. Instead, recognize when someone's pushing you. Stay strong, be smart, and don't lose your cool.

5. *Ignore put-downs.* If someone's putting you down, either to your face or behind your back, don't pay attention. Let people ruin their own reputations if they want to, but refuse to lower yourself to their level. Often others will lose interest when they see you're unaffected by their behavior.

6. *Use self-talk.* How we talk to ourselves can influence our actions and feelings when we're facing a tough choice. If you're feeling the stress of a difficult decision, you can say to yourself, "I'm feeling upset right now but I can stay calm and handle this situation in a positive way." Thinking you're in control can help you stay in control.

7. *Use I-messages.* If you're experiencing conflict with someone, instead of casting blame and potentially escalating conflicts, use I-messages as you work to resolve problems. I-messages work really well for presenting your case to authority figures. Instead of storming out of a classroom you might say something like, "I feel upset that I'm being blamed for what happened and would like to talk about it."

8. *Talk to someone.* Some situations benefit from another perspective. Talking through your decision with a good listener can help clarify things for you. Speak with a parent, teacher, or a trusted adult about anything that's giving you a hard time.

9. *Walk away.* Sometimes leaving is the best solution to a difficult situation. Split, boogie, depart, get out, hit the road. A little time and distance can provide the perspective you need. Most big challenges, of course, eventually will have to be addressed, but finding some time, space, and room to breathe in stressed moments can help you rethink a situation.

10. **Recognize when you're losing control.** Most of us have some sense of when we're feeling really upset and on the verge of doing something we'll regret. Try to recognize these feelings in yourself and take a break when you need one. When you're on your own, you might use focused breathing (page 44), positive self-talk, or another technique from this book to cool down.

Managing Peer Pressure

Does it sometimes seem like everyone thinks they know what's best for you? If it's not parents, it's friends—"You'll have fun at this party" or "You'll totally like this guy." And you might. But you also might not, and you might be put in a position where you feel pressure to do something you're not interested in or comfortable doing.

It's natural to want to be liked; nobody wants to be uncool, looked down on, or excluded. That's why peer pressure can be so persuasive. Here are some suggestions for standing your ground when the pressure's on.

1. **Play it straight.** Be pleasant, straightforward, and tell people what you don't want to do. Ask them to stop pressuring you. You can give a reason for your decision, but you don't have to explain yourself.

   "I don't want to smoke. End of discussion."

   "You can all go ahead. My mom's expecting me home."

2. **Offer another suggestion.** Offering an alternative can get you off the hot seat without risking a confrontation. As long as you're comfortable with the new idea, everyone can win.

   "I'm not really down for a fight with those guys tonight. Let's get something to eat instead."

   "I'm not going to write anything about Sara on my Web site. Let's put up a list of fashion tips instead."

3. **Make a joke or change the subject.** Joking or changing the topic of conversation can get you past some uncomfortable, pressure-packed moments. It's a gentle way to let someone know you're not interested in where the conversation or action is headed.

"No way. That stuff makes people act like zombies."

"Nah, I don't want to do that. But, hey, are you going to the game Thursday night?"

Sometimes even someone you are very close with will try to influence your thoughts and actions. If you're feeling a lot of pressure to behave in ways that make you uncomfortable, it's important to talk about it with that person. Describe the pressure you feel and what changes you'd like to happen. (You might use the ASSERT Formula on pages 60–65 for this discussion.) Good friends you trust will listen and accept your decisions.

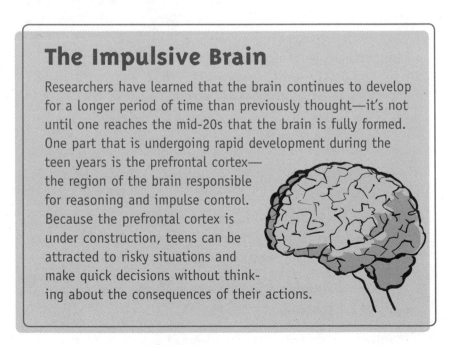

The Impulsive Brain

Researchers have learned that the brain continues to develop for a longer period of time than previously thought—it's not until one reaches the mid-20s that the brain is fully formed. One part that is undergoing rapid development during the teen years is the prefrontal cortex— the region of the brain responsible for reasoning and impulse control. Because the prefrontal cortex is under construction, teens can be attracted to risky situations and make quick decisions without thinking about the consequences of their actions.

Find Out More

Above the Influence (www.abovetheinfluence.com). Stories from real teens, games, and advice make this site a one-stop source of information for dealing with peer pressure.

The Complete Idiot's Guide to Surviving Peer Pressure for Teens **by Hilary Cherniss and Sara Jane Sluke.** This book looks at why teens feel being cool is so important and offers practical advice for handling peer-pressure situations that can come up at school or in your neighborhood.

The Courage to Be Yourself: True Stories by Teens About Cliques, Conflicts, and Overcoming Peer Pressure **edited by Al Desetta with Educators for Social Responsibility.** The 26 first-person stories in this book are all about making decisions during difficult times. Included are profiles of teens dealing with cliques, bullies, parent pressures, and more.

"I never knew how much control our thoughts have over how we feel. Now I use thinking to make myself feel better—not worse."
—**Mario, 16**

"When I need a lift, I go to funny Web sites. Having a good laugh can put things in perspective."
—**Amelia, 15**

"If you call yourself a loser all the time, you'll feel like a loser."
—**Aaron, 14**

"A positive attitude can make the difference between a good day and a really bad one."
—**Kelly, 13**

Choose the Upside View

Stress can make you feel anxious and eat away at your self-esteem. When you're at the limit of your ability to cope, it can seem like you're lost in the stress jungle and your life will never get better. But a few other skills can be helpful when it feels like invisible tigers are gaining on you. These techniques take almost no effort, are totally free, and have an instant payback. They're about making a choice to see the upside view of life.

Seeing the Upside

"Seeing the upside" means remembering all of the good things about you and your life. While this may sound too simple to be effective, it truly works. After all, stress is a reaction to the world you perceive—so, how you view and think about the world affects how you feel. Think about it: Have you ever been down or depressed about something, maybe even something small, and it grew and grew in your thoughts until it seemed like a huge problem for you to deal with? If you are full of anxious or frightened thoughts, it's easy to feel overwhelmed and out of control. Focusing on the negative is a sure way to become your own worst invisible stress tiger.

The opposite is true, too. When you have a positive attitude about yourself and your life, the world is a less stressful place. Instead of dwelling on the negative things that might happen, you can focus on your strengths and abilities to overcome challenges. It's true sad events or stressful situations will still occur and you'll have to deal with them, but when you can see the upside, the good things inside you, and the people who care about you, you're in a much stronger position to deal with tough times. That's why people often say that life is all about having the right attitude.

How do you begin to see the upside?

In the same way you strengthen your muscles by lifting weights, you can have a more positive attitude by practicing upside thoughts. Think about the great parts of your life and write them in a list. Include things you like and the people you care about. You might also list your talents, accomplishments, and anything else you appreciate or are proud of.

The Power of Positivity

Positive thinking has a powerful effect on your body. Research shows that people who are optimistic not only have better mental health, but also better physical health. Optimism can help your heart and lungs stay healthy and strengthen your immune system so that you are sick less often. It's even been shown that people with serious illnesses live longer when they have a sense of humor and a brighter outlook on life.

Things I'm Thankful For

a comfortable place to sleep at night

good food—especially pasta with pesto and mushrooms

my health

Mom and Dad

my science skills

my cat

my favorite hoodie

Tom, Ricardo, and the guys

my kindness toward others

our soccer team's domination

living in a free country

After you're done, take a close look at your list. It's important to recognize all of the things that are right with you and your life. Keep your list on hand and review it often. Add to it when new things come up.

Positive Self-Talk

We all talk to ourselves constantly, whether we realize it or not. If we actually had these conversations out loud, we might seem really weird—and we might not like hearing what comes out of our mouths. What we say to ourselves has a big impact on how we feel. Positive self-talk is another way to train yourself to choose the upside view.

Seeing the Positive

Instead of: "I'm so overweight. It's no wonder other kids tease me all the time."

Try: "I'm a good person and deserve to be treated with respect."

Instead of: "I'll never be able to improve my grades."

Try: "I'm smart and willing to work hard. I can work with my teachers to do better at school."

Instead of: "Other kids don't like me because I spazz out sometimes."

Try: "I have many good qualities and have a lot to share with others."

Instead of: "I'd like to try out for gymnastics but I'm no good."

Try: "I have a lot of determination and, with the coach's help, can succeed."

Instead of: "I can't do anything right and deserve to be miserable."

Try: "I'm a unique person with a lot of talents. I want and deserve a great life."

Instead of: "Things are out of control—I won't be able to get my life back on track."

Try: "I can handle my problems by making good decisions and getting help from others."

Replacing negative thoughts with positive ones can make a big difference in how you feel about yourself and your life. The key is to do it consistently—whenever you hear a negative thought in your head, replace it with a positive one. When you do, you can be your own best friend, build confidence, and tame invisible tigers.

Lighten Up

Another approach to seeing the upside is to see the humorous side of life. It's understandable that we're sometimes stressed or fearful about what's happening in our lives. And it's natural to be worried about troubling world events we learn about in the news. But always feeling anxious or afraid is unhealthy. That's why it's important to lighten up whenever we can—to smile and laugh and put things in perspective.

Scientists have known for a long time that humor has positive physical and emotional benefits. Laughter increases respiratory activity (breathing rate), oxygen exchange, muscular activity, and heart rate. It also stimulates the pituitary gland which leads to an overall positive biochemical state. Simply put, humor is good for you!

Sometimes it can be hard to laugh, like during very stressful periods or when something bad has happened. People who are very shy may also have a hard time showing a lighter side. You have the right to respond in your own way in these situations, but remember the old saying: Laughter is the best medicine. Here are some suggestions to lighten up.

Five Ways to Lighten Up

1. **Hang out with people who are happy and who have a good sense of humor.** Being around someone who's positive and funny can give you a lift. Make sure your personal safety net includes these people.

2. **Watch movies and TV shows you know will make you feel happy.** If you have a choice between a comedy or feel-good film and a movie that's very sad or disturbing, choose the one more likely to improve your spirits.

3. **Search the Internet for hilarious film clips and funny sites.** Spread the cheer by sharing what you find with family members and friends.

4. **Many people have a favorite comic strip or cartoon they like to read each day.** A variety of these can be found online.

5. **Learn one joke a week and share it with the people you know.** Even if some of the jokes are corny and cause groans from people, this habit can be a fun way to get others laughing—and to get them to share jokes of their own.

Seeing the upside view is important for feeling good about yourself. It helps you stay positive and keep things in perspective when life is particularly stressful or challenging. If you're skeptical, try using one of these methods for a day and see what happens. Learning to live on the upside can help you feel better in a hurry.

Find Out More

GoComics (www.gocomix.com). Visit this site to read many syndicated comic strips including *Calvin and Hobbes, Go Team Bob!,* and many more. You can even have cartoons emailed to you every day.

TeensHealth (www.teenshealth.org). TeensHealth has advice for keeping your mind and body in tip-top shape. You'll find information on dealing with tough situations, staying positive, and getting help when you need it.

"I'm afraid of failing or not being good enough."

"I try, but I'll never be able to do everything I'm supposed to do."

"I'm always tired. I feel like I'm getting sick."

"The only way out is to just get away from it all."

"I'm not happy with myself or what I'm doing."

"I feel alone with my problems, like nobody cares or understands."

"I have no idea where my life is going and I don't care anymore."

First Aid for Tiger Bites

It's frightening to feel at the limit of what you can handle. First of all, remember that you're not alone. Many people feel overwhelmed, scared, lost, or depressed during difficult times. The important thing is to recognize when you need help and act in positive ways to help yourself feel better.

When Is It Time to Get Help?

Knowing the signs of stress overload is important so you know when to reach out for help. Here are the signals:

Always feeling angry. If it seems like you're mad a lot of the time, built-up tension could be affecting your mood. You might also get into more arguments with teachers, classmates, and people in your house.

Changes in sleeping habits. If you're under a lot of pressure, you might have trouble getting or staying asleep. Or maybe you want to sleep all of the time. Problems with sleep are one way your body tells you something is wrong.

Changes in eating habits. Stress can affect appetite. Some people experiencing anxiety lose their appetite. Others want to eat everything in sight. Eating and feeling full can change your body chemistry and temporarily mask the effects of stress.

Aches, pains, and increased sickness. Ongoing stress weakens the immune system and can cause a variety of health problems. Some health concerns that are often stress-related include headaches, stomachaches, sore muscles, colds, and infections.

Escapist behaviors. Overdoing things like TV, listening to music, exercising, playing video games, surfing the Internet, studying, and sleeping can mean you're stuck in a vicious circle of stress avoidance (see page 13). Hours and hours of these activities not only causes you to miss out on other fun experiences, but also adds to the stress you feel.

Withdrawing from family members and friends. Always wanting to be alone is a very serious sign that something is wrong. It's when you're feeling your worst that you most need the important people in your life.

Feeling nervous, frightened, or worried all the time. Stress can make you feel constantly on edge—like something bad could happen any moment. Some people even experience panic attacks, which are sudden feelings of overwhelming anxiety that come without warning or any obvious reason. These feelings can wear you down and suck up so much of your energy that even everyday tasks become difficult to handle.

Crying often and for no apparent reason. Crying when you're upset about an event is normal and a positive way to process sad feelings. But if you find yourself feeling sad, hopeless, or crying a lot, it's time to get help.

Using alcohol or other drugs. Drinking alcohol, smoking cigarettes, or using other drugs are definite signals that a person needs help. These substances harm your body and ultimately make you feel worse.

Feeling out of control. For many people on stress overload, the world seems to spin faster and faster until they feel they can no longer hang on. It's a terrifying feeling that generates its own stress.

Feeling depressed or wanting to harm yourself. Not being able to handle all the challenges in your life can lead to depression, unhealthy risks, and self-harming behaviors. If you feel hopeless about life or like you want to hurt yourself, talk to someone right away.

Things to Remember...

Desperate thinking and self-destructive behaviors are signals you need help, support, and objectivity from people you trust. Here are some things to keep in mind as you work to heal tiger bites:

1. It's okay to admit you need help. One of the biggest challenges can be admitting we're in trouble. It's often hard to acknowledge life isn't working out or that we've made some bad decisions. But not admitting that we're having difficulties—to ourselves or others—is denial. Denial allows us to fool ourselves into thinking we're handling things better than we really are. To really feel better, it's important to admit we need help. It can take real courage and strength, but it's the only doorway to a better life.

2. People you trust want to help. When we're struggling with challenges, it can seem like we're troubling others by opening up and sharing with them. This thinking leads to feeling more and more isolated over time. Don't let this keep you from reaching out in your time of greatest need. Parents, other family members, friends, spiritual leaders, school counselors, teachers, and other people you trust want to support you. They can provide a safe environment where you have permission to be your mixed-up, confused, lost, or even weird self. People we trust accept us no matter what and can help us find ways to overcome challenges. If one person doesn't seem to take your worries seriously or to be able to help, reach out to another. Don't stop reaching out until someone takes your concerns seriously.

Important!

If you don't feel like there's anyone you can talk to, call the Girls and Boys Town National Hotline (1-800-448-3000). This hotline is staffed with people who want to help.

3. Stop negative coping behaviors. Coping behaviors help us avoid uncomfortable feelings that come with the difficult challenges. But they are only short-term solutions that can make things worse and don't address the root problems causing stress. Negative coping behaviors (like isolating yourself or using alcohol or other drugs) are destructive. Stopping them is important for feeling better. Maybe some people around you make it difficult to stop these behaviors. Reach out to others you trust who can help. Failure is not in making mistakes, but in not learning from them and making smarter choices the next time you're faced with the same challenge.

4. Plan to deal with personal issues. At some point, many of us will have to deal with tough times in life. Whether it's a problem with drinking or violence at home, abuse, the death of a family member or friend, a disability, or any other difficult situation, it's important to address what's going on. If you feel like you can't control what's happening, you can start to feel terrified, confused, ashamed, sad, or hopeless. Don't wait until that happens. Reach out for the help and support you need as soon as you need it.

A Final Word

I hope what you've learned about stress and the ways you can handle it will make the "jungle" of your life less threatening and easier to get through. Have the courage to dream big dreams, treat yourself well, and go after what you really want. You deserve the very best. By taking great care of yourself and using the life skills in this book, you can put together an amazing life.

My best wishes go with you.

Earl Hipp

Index

Other Great Books from Free Spirit!

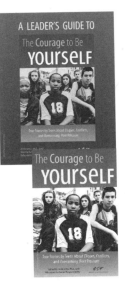

Mad
How to Deal with Your Anger and Get Respect
by James J. Crist, Ph.D.

Feeling mad is a normal human emotion. But some teens go too far. Their anger controls them and affects their lives in negative, sometimes long-lasting ways. This practical, supportive book helps teens learn why we get angry and how anger affects our bodies and relationships. Tools and strategies help them control their anger and avoid poor decisions and actions; insights from real teens let them know they're not alone. Mental health problems that can complicate anger management and the role of counseling and psychotherapy are explored. Includes resources. For ages 13 & up.

160 pp., softcover, 2-color, illust., 6" x 9"

The Struggle to Be Strong
True Stories by Teens About Overcoming Tough Times
edited by Al Desetta, M.A., of Youth Communication, and Sybil Wolin, Ph.D., of Project Resilience

In 30 first-person accounts, teens tell how they overcame major life obstacles. As teens read this book, they will discover they're not alone in facing life's difficulties. They'll also learn about seven resiliencies—insight, independence, relationships, initiative, creativity, humor, and morality—that everyone needs to overcome tough times. For ages 13 & up.

192 pp., softcover, illust., 6" x 9"

Leader's Guide
by Sybil Wolin, Ph.D., of Project Resilience, and Al Desetta, M.A., and Keith Hefner of Youth Communication

For teachers, social workers, case workers, clinicians, prevention specialists, counselors, and other adults who work with youth in grades 7–12.

176 pp., softcover, 8½" x 11"

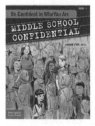

Be Confident in Who You Are
Middle School Confidential™, Book 1
by Annie Fox, M.Ed.

The first book in the Middle School Confidential series follows Jack, Jen, Chris, Abby, Mateo, and Michelle as they work to meet new challenges and survive the social scene—without losing sight of who they are. Readers get information on common challenges and practical advice for being healthy, feeling good about who they are, and staying in control of feelings and actions—even when the pressure is on. Features graphic-novel-style illustrations, quotes, quizzes, tips, tools, and resources. For ages 11–14.

96 pp., softcover, color illust., 6" x 8"

Too Stressed to Think?
A Teen Guide to Staying Sane When Life Makes You Crazy
by Annie Fox, M.Ed., and Ruth Kirschner

When stress has the "survival brain" on overdrive, what happens to the "thinking brain"? How can teens stay cool and make smart choices when the pressure's on? This book is packed with stress-lessening tools teens can use every day. Scenarios describe situations readers can relate to. Each is followed by a process for reducing or stopping the stress and making sound decisions. Quotes from real teens remind stressed-out readers that they're not alone. Includes resources. For ages 12 & up.

176 pp., softcover, illust., 6" x 9"

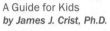

What to Do When You're Scared & Worried
A Guide for Kids
by James J. Crist, Ph.D.

Advice, reassurance, and strategies kids can use to recognize, understand, and manage their fears, plus guidance on getting help for hard-to-handle problems they can't manage on their own. For ages 9–13.

128 pp., 2-color, illust., softcover, 5³/₈" x 8³/₈"

The Kids' Guide to Working Out Conflicts
How to Keep Cool, Stay Safe, and Get Along
by Naomi Drew, M.A.

Proven ways to avoid conflict and defuse tough situations, written by an expert on conflict resolution and peacemaking. Kids learn how to stand up for themselves without getting physical, how to talk out problems, how to de-stress and calm down, how to deal with teasing and bullying, how to stay safe, and more—essential life skills for all young people. For ages 10–14.

160 pp., softcover, 7" x 9"

For pricing information, to place an order, or to request a free catalog, contact:

Free Spirit Publishing Inc.
217 Fifth Avenue North • Suite 200 • Minneapolis, MN 55401-1299
toll-free 800.735.7323 • local 612.338.2068 • fax 612.337.5050
help4kids@freespirit.com • www.freespirit.com

31901046212835